The Heartbeat *of the* Year

The Heartbeat of the Year

The Epistles of the Act of Consecration

GÜNTHER DELLBRÜGGER

Floris Books

Translated by Mary Graham

Bible quotations are from the New International Version
Cover image: *Schöpfung (Creation)* by Ninetta Sombart
Used with kind permission

First published in German as *Im Herzland: Zur Esoterik des christlichen Jahres* by Verlag Urachhaus, Stuttgart in 2014, second edition 2020
First published in English by Floris Books, Edinburgh in 2025
© 2014, 2020 Verlag Freies Geistesleben & Urachhaus GmbH
English version © 2025 Floris Books

Günther Dellbrügger has asserted his right under the Copyright, Design and Patents Act 1988 to be identified as the Author of this Work
All rights reserved. No part of this book may be reproduced in any form without written permission of Floris Books, Edinburgh
www.florisbooks.co.uk

Authorised EU Representative: Easy Access System Europe,
Mustamae tee 50, 10621 Tallinn, Estonia gpsr.requests@easproject.com
British Library CIP Data available
ISBN 978-178250-966-0

In grateful memory of Rudolf Frieling (1901–86)

Contents

Foreword *by Tom Ravetz* — 11

Preface — 15

1.
God's Word in the Sacramental Word — 17

2.
Entrance and Exit — 21

3. Trinity
The Trinitarian Human Being — 26

4. Advent
Set Forth, Become Light — 34

5. Christmas
Christ of All the Earth — 53

6. Epiphany
The Star of Grace — 68

7. Passiontide
Know Yourself — 78

8. Easter
In the Realm of the Heart — 88

9. Ascension
Traces of Heaven and Traces of Earth   100

10. Pentecost
Flame of Spirit   106

11. St John's Tide
Christ's Light in the Light of Day   111

12. Michaelmas
The Heart's Journey to Christ   121

13.
Veins of Gold   138

Contemplations on the Epistles   141
Rudolf Frieling
- *On the seasonal prayers (1926)* — *141*
- *The basic epistle (1963)* — *144*
- *The Trinity epistle (1974)* — *145*
- *Passiontide (1963)* — *146*
- *Easter (1963)* — *148*
- *Ascension (1963)* — *152*
- *St John's Tide (1963)* — *158*
- *Michaelmas (1963)* — *164*
- *The altar in the epistles (1963)* — *169*

The Epistles and Inserted Prayers   175
   North American and British versions

Notes   209

Bibliography   223

A mystery is something that provides continuous food for thought.

Eric-Emmanuel Schmitt

Foreword

The Translations of the Ritual Texts

Any act of understanding involves a kind of translation: we hear or read words that someone has spoken or written, coming from their own world of memories and concerns, and bring them into relationship with ourselves. In this sense, the meaning that we find in what we read or hear is a new creation, representing what the speaker or author meant in our terms. When it comes to translating from one language into another, this task of taking in the original and recreating it is all the clearer. In *Growing Point,* Alfred Heidenreich writes:

> A very responsible and challenging task was the "Englishing" of our rituals. An attempt had to be made, however imperfectly, to enter into the mysterious field where words have their origin in creative ideas and whence these ideas issue forth into the spoken form of a living language.

This makes it clear that translating our ritual texts cannot be a question of simply looking up a German word or phrase in the dictionary and writing down the equivalent English word. Some of the great translations of poetry demonstrate this. Take, for example, the translation of the *Duino Elegies* by Sir Stephen Spender. If we put the English translation into an online translation site, the German that comes out is quite different from Rilke's original. Nevertheless, the new work of art that Spender created comes from the same spirit as the original.

In this sense, there can never be a definitive and final 'right' translation. We are always feeling our way towards a deeper understanding of the German texts, in order to sense that world beyond language where living concepts reside; then we are trying to find the words that work in the English language that can best convey these concepts in a way that can be understood. Just as Rudolf Steiner had to choose German words that were understandable in the context of his day when he brought the words of the rituals from the spiritual world, we have to find words that work for English speakers' ears.

The original translation of the rituals was made by A.C. Harwood and Alfred Heidenreich in order to found The Christian Community in Britain. When other English-speaking regions were established, they took over the British translation. It is perhaps fair to say that the English of that original version reflected the cultural background of A.C. Harwood and the liturgical language of that time. For example, while 'thee', 'thou' and 'thine' are grammatically more correct as a rendering of *Du* and *Dein,* the fact that these words were used only for church purposes in English does not reflect the usage in German.

As The Christian Community in North America grew stronger, some of these usages began to jar. A new translation of the rituals was undertaken starting in the 1970s. Although the body of the Act of Consecration is largely the same, the translation of the epistles used in North America is different from that used in Britain. Responsibility for the translations used in the respective regions has been given over to the regional synods; however, the regions compare their versions and strive for unity where possible. The translations used in the Australia and New Zealand region and in the Southern Africa region are different again. Even the name of the central ritual is different – the Act of Consecration of Man in Britain and Southern Africa, the Consecration of the Human Being in North America, and the Act of Consecration of the Human Being in Australia and New Zealand.

Some readers may be encountering the fact that we have different translations in the different regions for the first time. They may find the texts that are quoted in the body of the book are unfamiliar. Perhaps, with the thoughts of this foreword in mind, they might find it stimulating to perceive the same meaning, rendered in different ways, as can be fruitful when studying a Bible passage.

For the translation of Günther Dellbrügger's book we have chosen the version that is used in the North American region for the simple reason that the book is likely to find the most readers in that part of the world. At the end of the book, the epistles are shown in both the North American and the British versions.

Tom Ravetz
Lenker of The Christian Community in
Great Britain and Ireland

Preface

Ritual texts exist to be read aloud and heard. The author does not therefore intend this book to be a substitute for the 'live' experience. It is rather intended to be a companion for people who want to participate actively in the renewed sacrament of The Christian Community out of a deepened spiritual awareness and understanding.

Today, there is a growing need to move beyond religious experience and to acquire knowledge of the spirit: 'The time has now come when ... a person with true religious feelings is driven by these very feelings to seek knowledge.'[1]

The seasonal prayers or epistles of the Act of Consecration, the Consecration of the Human Being, were published in German in 1994 as part of the collected works of Rudolf Steiner and are now also available on the internet.[2] I consider it useful to print the epistles in full in this book. Readers are asked to find their own responsible way of handling the epistle texts.

> If individuals receiving the sacraments live in them
> with full consciousness, they will be continually healed
> by them.[3]

Günther Dellbrügger

1.

God's Word in the Sacramental Word

In the Act of Consecration, we experience images, words and actions or deeds. When we cross the threshold into the chapel for the service, we enter into the *image* of the divine world that lives invisibly in our world. The *word*, through which we reforge our connection to the divine world, resounds in this image-world, in the light of the seven candles. The *deed* of the Offertory, the event of the Transubstantiation and the grace of the Communion all flow from the living Word.

This book is primarily concerned with the activity of the Word throughout the festive prayers or epistles of The Christian Community. Though they often reference a certain historical event or time, these prayers relate to the present, speaking to whatever our current destiny and life situation may be. For example, the words referring to the death of Jesus Christ two thousand years ago become a mirror for our self-knowledge in the Passion weeks: 'O human soul, empty is the place of your heart,' while the resurrection of Jesus Christ at Easter becomes our own resurrection: 'Living is the soul which was dead.' Christ's deeds take place anew on the wings of the ritual words.

In the Middle Ages a distinction was made with respect to how the ritual text should come *through* the priest *(per sacerdotem)*, rather than *from* the priest *(ex sacerdote)*. Similarly, the ideal for how the words should come *through* the priest during the sacrament is formulated in the Ordination service in the following way: may the celebrant 'speak and live in the speaking and living of Christ'.

In a lecture in Berlin in 1917, Rudolf Steiner described Jesus Christ's speaking in a wonderful way. This valuable description belongs in the truest sense of the word to the *Building Stones for an Understanding of the Mystery of Golgotha* – which is the title of that lecture series – and offers the opportunity to feel how Christ himself can live in the Word, and in so doing, raise the Word back up to its source.

Steiner described the unique experience of the early Christians that arose through the ability of the apostles to impart the sound and the tone of Christ's own speech. More significant than the content of the teaching was 'the sound, this quite distinctive quality of the way that Christ Jesus spoke'.[1] A magical power was inherent in his words – an elementary force that gripped the listeners like no other. Although Christ Jesus had to express himself in the language of his listeners, the primal language that was once common to all beings on earth lived in his soul, and this 'inner Word' came through his speech as an undifferentiated power. This power can live in a human being 'who is fully inspired by the Word', the Logos. Christ was and is this Logos, with which he identifies himself completely and through which he works. His words carry the warming power of the sun.

According to Rudolf Steiner, we can essentially distinguish three epochs in the historical human relationship to language and our ability to speak. In ancient times, people felt *beauty* in the qualities of the sounds and the flow of the sentences, and strove to speak beautifully. From the time of the Greeks, and in particular the Romans, through the Enlightenment to this day, one endeavours for *truth* and logically correct speech. The aesthetic form alone can even be perceived as one-sided when describing 'outer beauty' or 'mere appearance'. The task of the future with regards to speaking will be to develop *good* speech, or right speaking, as it could be referred to in English. In a lecture in 1921, Steiner described in surprising detail that the essential characteristic of right speech is that the speaker is *in right relationship* with what and how one speaks. This implies that right speaking goes beyond mere logical correctness and entails speaking from the context of life:

> To let a pronouncement or the like arise at a particular place out of a living relationship, that is what leads over from beauty, from correctness, to the ethos of language – at which one feels, when a sentence is uttered, whether one may or may not say it in the whole context ... This is what I should like to call good speaking or bad speaking.[2]

The sacrament itself is a high schooling for right speech. The priest endeavours to make the ritual texts sound like events from the world of the hierarchies so that Christ himself can live into and work through them. Insofar as the priest is the representative of humanity, however, the sacrament takes place through them *in connection* with humanity, with the Trinity, and with the development of the world. Their speaking paves the way for the 'becoming of the world':

> I always find it extremely humorous when well-meaning people say all the time that words don't matter, deeds do! ...
> Everything that happens in the world in regard to actions depends on words! One who can see through things knows that nothing takes place that hasn't been prepared in advance by somebody through words.[3]

When the divine Word comes to life in the ritual words as spoken by a human being, right speech arises out of a future grace. This right speech paves the way for right action, thereby leading to progress in the world in line with Christ's spiritual goals. The more people are able to develop a sense for this right speech of the sacrament, the stronger and more fundamental an effect it will have on our actions. In that way, this right speech can become a preparatory force for the future.[4]

The epistle texts printed in this book are at first glance just words on paper, like a score composed for the sacred event. May the reader, in absorbing what is written, practise inward listening. May the experience lead to inner participation, creating space for the healing salvation expressed through image, word and deed in the sacrament.

The invention of printing brought both loss and gain – loss particularly with respect to religious life. Since then, the gospel is no longer aurally received as a divine message embedded in the events at the altar, but has become a text among texts. The Bible became the book of books for many, but a book nonetheless. As such, it brought the possibility of independent study and critique, the chance to delve deeper, to discover parts never heard before. Who today would want to give up the freedom to read the gospel for themselves? On the other hand, religious experience can become more difficult to attain, and textual criticism can become like clouds obscuring the heavenly light of the gospel.

Today we are at the point in the history of humanity where we can recognise that the printed word has given us freedom, but at the same time has also presented us with tasks in relation to the gospel and the epistles. We can ask ourselves the following:

— What is special or characteristic about this text?
— Can I learn to read and hear between the lines of what is now being spoken to me? For example, what do I hear in the words 'He is risen, he is not here'?
— Can I reawaken that which has solidified into printed words on paper? Can I infuse with living meaning what has become fixed?[5]

In this way, the presumed loss can become a great gain, for people today need spiritual knowledge in order to find a new approach to religion. With an awake and deepened sense of our individual interiority, we can animate and affirm the words of the sacrament, becoming co-celebrants. This is what the explanations of this book would like to contribute to and inspire.

2.

Entrance and Exit

The epistles are the bookends of the Consecration of the Human Being in that they are heard at the beginning and end of the service. The priest speaks them on the righthand side, the side of activity, where the Offertory – when we lift our will, feelings and thinking towards the divine – is also performed. The epistles affect our will, our feeling, and our thinking, sometimes the one more than the other. As what lives in the soul is raised up and transformed, out of the spiritualised soul arises the spirit self. This is expressed as a plea at the end of the Trinity epistle where it says,

May he fill with spirit all the ways of our human soul.

It is worth noting here that the use of 'our' implies not only those physically present, but also the circle of those who belong to the church but are not present at that moment, as well as all those who have a sense for it and who may soon join in. The circle of participants grows like the ever-widening ripples after an object falls into the water – and yet there is talk of one soul in which all are united: 'May he fill ... our human *soul*' – not *souls*.

The way to understand how the deep meaning of the epistles is linked to the spiritualisation of the soul is to walk with the risen Christ as he reveals himself to us. Speaking with Friedrich Rittelmeyer, Rudolf Steiner once said that even if all the documents of Christianity were destroyed, one would still be able to find Christ in the experience of the rhythm of the seasons. In a similar way, insofar as they free Christ from the confines of all that is confessional and conventional, the epistles allow us to experience how Christ is there for *all* people.

We experience time on different levels: we experience the rhythm of the day through our body, particularly through the meals in the morning, at midday and in the evening. Our soul, on the other hand, moves with the seasons: we experience an urge to expand on all levels in spring and summer, and by contrast, an inclination towards concentration and solitude in autumn and winter.

The cycle of Christian festivals lends new accents to this experience of nature, highlighting aspects that are, in fact, independent of external nature. These aspects consist of encounters between the human soul and the soul of the Christ-being that is living with us, which we could also call the soul of the world. In Christ himself we can also distinguish the different aspects of his being: the mystery of his body, which he wrested from death for all of us in his resurrection; the mystery of his soul, which was and is ready for the great sacrifice ('... and uniting his soul therewith'); and finally, the Christ-spirit, his actual innermost being, his I, in which all his impulses for action originate.

These prayers guide us through the festivals of the year in a way that engages our soul space. They lift us into the soul realm of Christ and allow us to immerse ourselves in it – what grace! That is the realm of encounter, where we feel him and his ministering angelic beings looking upon us.

Like a gardener building up the soil before planting seeds, we can prepare ourselves for this encounter by cultivating the right inner condition of soul, which is an act that we ourselves have to perform on and with our soul. The opening words of the Act of Consecration and the fundamental motives it expresses guide us into this soul-preparation. The first thing we hear is that we are gathered in order to do something together, and to fulfil it worthily.

Some basic thoughts of Aristotle are illuminating regarding the intrinsic character of what we are to accomplish together. He

2. ENTRANCE AND EXIT

formulated the distinction between theory and practice. 'Theory' is the vision of the idea, for instance, the idea of good, of justice, of beauty. The word 'theory' contains the word for God, *theos*, indicating that theory is an experience of the *essence* of the thing – theory is 'divine vision', whereas 'practice' is the realisation of an idea in external reality. An idea becomes a motive for action, and I can implement this idea and manifest it in our material world by creating something.

In the context of the sacrament, the idea of an altar as a place of prayer and sacrifice is the theory, actually building the altar is the practice.

What about the actual act at the altar? Aristotle also writes – albeit not extensively – of a third, intermediary element that comes between and overlaps both theory and practice. Taking the example of the altar, this third element is, on the one hand, an action whose purpose arises from the 'theory', from the concept of the altar as a meeting place between God and human beings, and on the other hand, it is an act that takes place in space and time, involving physical objects and materials: a chalice, bread and wine. Aristotle calls this mysterious mediation *poiesis*, or creation. Creation thus moves between and overlaps both theory and practice. In our context, this refers to the enacting of the service. The living encounter between God and human beings takes place in a practical sense at the external altar via the spirit-infused *poiesis* or *creation*, consisting of the words, gestures and actions. We see the colours of the vestments, the room in the light of the altar candles, we hear the words spoken – as much as the event is enacted, it is also *revealed*.

The epistle texts in particular are pure *poiesis:* they create the spiritual meeting space, summoning the divine from the realm of ideas – each time anew – and allowing the colours of the soul to come into being in space and time throughout the cycle of the festivals. Christ as Lord of the Earth mediates between the realm of the divine and the sphere of earth activity, living and weaving between the two. He is the true divine creator, the heavenly 'poet'. Through the epistles we are allowed to participate in the work of this poet, celebrate and praise him, ask him to draw near, experience his stern but always loving gaze on us. The epistles are colours and music, sound and silence in the kingdom of Christ. They invite us to encounter the divine, each time anew. These opening words of the service are the gate through which we enter into the sacrament, or a garment we put on in order to enter worthily into the heavenly kingdom of the entire sacramental revelation of Christ. We enter Christ's revelation – as if entering a cathedral – out of the deepest veneration of Christ, which we can only muster through devotion to his deed on Golgotha.

Calling the bookend texts of the Act of Consecration 'epistles' can remind us of the epistles in the New Testament. It is a true comparison in the sense that they are also messages from the divine world that are relevant for our time. Like Paul's letters, they also express concrete spiritual facts, as in 'Christ has risen to you as the meaning of the earth'; and challenge us to spiritual deeds, as in 'Know this …'; or offer us an austere mirror, as in 'Empty is the place of your heart'. Taking this seriously and understanding it as spiritually relevant for our lives today may set us on a rollercoaster of emotions. At the very least, it sets the soul in motion, perhaps leading to new and deeper experiences.

The length of time for which we hear any given epistle varies. There are texts that we hear spoken only once a year (midnight and dawn at Christmas); others, three times a year (the three Pentecost days); some, for more than four weeks (Epiphany, St John's, Michaelmas); and one that we may listen to for forty days (Easter). In some cases, we can have great moments of insight in which we briefly glimpse what a particular epistle is expressing. We should receive these gifts of insight with the greatest attention. In other cases, there are texts that we settle into over a longer period of time. These become life companions for us, growing on us as the meaning of their precious, ingenious words dawns on us gradually. We absorb them through our consciousness into our body, and thus begin to live with the spiritual realm.

2. ENTRANCE AND EXIT

The epistles give the unchanging text of the Act of Consecration a certain tint, just as the changing sacramental colours on the altar and vestments each lend a different character to the Consecration. The epistles are the entrance and exit, the alpha and omega of the service. They open and close the sacred Act of Consecration of the Human Being, and at the end, dismiss us with their blessing. Again and again, these words touch us with the divine world, so that we may carry Christianity with us, allowing it to permeate our lives.

In this sense, we can grow into these motivating words from Paul to the Corinthians: 'You are a letter from Christ' (2Cor 3:3). At the same time, Paul reveals the tension that characterises our human nature: 'For I do not do the good I want to do, but the evil I do not want to do – this I keep on doing' (Rom 7:19). These two statements depict two poles between which our humanity is stretched. Everyone can experience this existential stretching for themselves, and the moment one recognises the truth of it is the moment one begins a path to true self-knowledge.

That was the path that Paul also walked, which is how he was able to offer us these words as guiding stars, words that reveal our true future that slumbers in our soul like a seed. As if spoken by Christ himself, these words call out to the true humanity within us:

> You are God's field, God's building. (1Cor 3:9)
> Don't you know that you yourselves are God's temple and that God's Spirit dwells in your midst? (1Cor 3:16)
> Now you are the body of Christ. (1Cor 12:27)
> You are all one in Christ Jesus. (Gal 3:28)
> Then you will shine among them like stars in the sky. (Phil 2:15)
> You are all children of the light and children of the day. (1Th 5:5)

The Act of Consecration is a path to these starry goals of our humanity. It consecrates us into our future.[1]

3. Trinity

The Trinitarian Human Being

We encounter the Trinitarian principle in the basic epistle during the Trinity festival periods, but it also permeates the entire Act of Consecration, insofar as it is revealed in the words that accompany the three signs of the cross that take place seven times throughout the service:

The Father God be in us.
The Son God create in us.
The Spirit God enlighten us.

Contemplating the three signs of the cross will lead to deeper insight into the basic epistle. What is expressed in the words and in this ritual gesture of crossing oneself? Something sublime and wonderful happens through this act, particularly when it is accompanied by the words above: it allows us as individual human beings to relate directly to the Trinity.

There are three parts to this action: the naming of the triune Godhead, the plurality of community expressed in the words: '... be in *us*, ... create in *us*, ... enlighten *us*,' and finally, the signs of the cross itself, which we perform individually. In this action there is a working together of the divine Trinity, the congregation – those physically present, all true Christians who have been born, and those who have died – as well as the individuals who actively seek to realise their own Christianity. The sign of the cross that the priest in vestments makes includes the *whole* congregation. (A priest not in vestments makes three crosses like every member of the congregation.)

3. TRINITY: THE TRINITARIAN HUMAN BEING

The individual signs of the cross relate to three parts of our body, even if we do not touch them directly when performing the three crosses. These are the places that are touched during baptism: the forehead, the chin and the chest. Crossing ourselves at these three places is like renewing the Baptism on an individual level.

Let us visualise the intentions of the baptismal ceremony as it happens in The Christian Community: during the sacrament, water is placed on the forehead, salt on the chin, and ashes on the chest. How can we understand these three substances more deeply? One of the first things we hear about the substances is a negative statement in the sacramental text. For each substance, we first hear, 'This is not ...' Then we are asked to identify the substances that appear before us in their ordinary, external form – water, salt and ash – and transform them in our thoughts back into their origin. In the case of water, for example, we are called to think of it as 'the Spirit's all-permeating power'.

In the course of the Baptism, the Father is connected with the substance of the world, the Son with the stream of the Word, and the Spirit with the radiance of light. In this way the qualities of the persons of the Trinity are revealed in an archetypal way, but the other two also resonate in each of these three qualities. Thus, for example, the substance of the world comes into being through the principle of the creating Word, and this is a process in which the whole thing catches a glimpse of 'the light of the world'. Substance of the world, stream of the Word, and radiance of light, which from our perspective appear separate, work together and are united as one in the divine realm.

It becomes clear from all of this that our thinking must 'learn to dance' if it wants to reach the primordial sphere from which all forms of matter have emerged. In the Baptism, the divine blessing of the Trinity works out of this sphere into the physical human body, mediated through the substances reconnected with their origin.

With this in mind, the action of making the three crosses can be understood in a completely new light, namely as a continuation of the spiritual impulse that was imprinted in the whole human being with water, salt and ash.

In making the three crosses, we ask for the blessing of the Father for our existence, the blessing of the Son for our creative activity, and the blessing of the Spirit for the illumination of our consciousness. In this way we open our inner being consciously to the forces from which the world emerged. The Baptism, the three crosses, and the Trinity epistle all help to awaken us and enable us to take up our true task: in following Christ, to wrest not only ourselves but also the world from the death of matter. When we can permeate ourselves with the forces of the Trinity and make ourselves available as a tool for these forces, we become a growing point for divine creation.

The placement of the Trinity epistle at the beginning of the Consecration of the Human Being orients the sacrament to the strengthening of human beings. This epistle offers us a glimpse into the 'holy remnant' of divine creation in every human being.

> *Conscious of our humanity, we feel the divine Father.*
> *He is in all that we are.*
> *Our substance is his substance.*
> *Our being is his being.*
> *He moves in us through all existence.*

'Our humanity' encompasses not only quantitatively all people, but also the essence of being human. Our entire being has its origin in God the Father. Waking up to this spiritual fact means regaining awareness of our spiritual origin.

When Christ was approaching the end of his earthly life, united with God, he said, 'I am going to the Father.' He uttered this statement as the Son of God who became human, thereby giving us the opportunity to return to the Father and also to develop such a relationship with him. Becoming aware of how we humans are connected to God the Father through both substance and being can lead to an experience of deep gratitude.

3. TRINITY: THE TRINITARIAN HUMAN BEING

With the second verse, the Christ verse, we enter a completely different dimension. The Father consciousness sheds light on our divine origin from our distant past, which, though still hidden, shines into our present. The experience of the Son leads us into the present. We step from the comprehensive, divine experience of space into time, into change and development, for Christ is the God of time. In him we have a divine guide for our human development, complete with all its dynamics and drama. This part of the epistle also illuminates the proximity of Christ to us human beings.

> *Aware of the Christ in our humanity, we feel the divine Son.*

To be able to perceive the working of Christ in our life and creative activity, it is necessary to develop an organ of perception. This process happens unconsciously through the myriad crises that every human being faces – struggles that lead us to those painful but precious moments in which we feel asked not about the development of our outer life, not about our preferences nor about our abilities and characteristics, but about our very core: *who are you, really?* Shaken by the crisis, cast away and on our own, these are the moments when we can feel our innermost core open up.

Christ reaches us in our most vulnerable moments when we have come to our limits; he finds us most easily when all we ordinarily hide behind falls away. The question, 'How do I find Christ?' has a simple answer: 'By opening myself to him.' The fact that we are allowed to feel the divine Son in our humanity is a healing grace of destiny to which we can and must awaken.

Today, all people carry within them the treasure of a prenatal encounter with Christ. Before being born, each of us met him as the lord of heavenly forces on earth. We then forget this in order to become citizens of the earth and to find on our own the answer to Christ's question: 'Who do you say I am?' (Mk 8:29). Plato once saw every act of cognition as a re-cognition – a moment when we become aware of something again that we once knew but have forgotten. In this sense, the epistle encourages us to explore whether there is a hidden resonance within when Christ is spoken of as the divine Son, or when we hear of his reign in the world, of his life and activity in us, or of his dynamic proximity in all the processes of our soul's moving and becoming.

> *He wields through the world as Spirit-Word.*
> *He creates in all that we create.*
> *Our existing is his creating.*
> *Our life is his creating life.*
> *He creates through us in all the soul's creating.*

In this way we will gradually learn to experience the living, creative Christ in ourselves and in the world. We will increasingly experience that the epistle opens up to us the inner dimension of our everyday life: the activity of the one who revealed himself in the words: 'I am the life.'

The Father is more about rediscovering the divine primal being, whereas with respect to Christ, we have the task of perceiving the one who is always becoming, indeed, who is the activity of becoming itself. This is a great task of cognition, because involuntarily we always want to 'fix' something in our cognition. But when something is by its very nature in flux, such as water, I can analyse it chemically, but what does that mean? The result can certainly be 'correct' while at the same time being far removed from the living fullness of the truth itself.

Participating in the sacrament can realign our view of our own life, give forces of uprightness and rekindle faith. However, our faith today can and must be supported by clear spiritual discernment.

The third part of the epistle speaks of the work of the Holy Spirit. Through Christ – as the Creed puts it – can the healing Spirit work. He works in *true thinking*. In the Gospel of John (8:32), Christ says: 'And the truth will set you free.' We are called upon

3. TRINITY: THE TRINITARIAN HUMAN BEING

to use this true thinking to discern the spirits at work here. What stands out here is the focus on human freedom. On the path leading to human dignity, there is a fine line between the lack of freedom and pseudo-freedom. The salvation of true thinking lies in the discernment of the spirits that rule these different possibilities.

The power received through Christ now becomes spiritually fruitful. We urgently need this help, considering that our civilisation today carries a strong materialistic impulse to deny the spirit. The theoretical materialism that emerged in the nineteenth century has long since become practical materialism. A 'spirituality' is at work here, too, but one that only appeals to and incites the egoism hidden in every human being.

Up to this point, the Trinity epistle speaks in indicative sentences: The divine Father *is* in all that we are. Christ, the divine Son, *wields* through the world as the Spirit-Word, creating in and through us, and so on. The third verse of the Trinity epistle also begins with an indicative sentence, which expresses a spiritual reality. With the grasping of the spirit, however, our participation with the divine increases, for in order to grasp the spirit, we must rise to the spirit realm. We can do this through the power of Christ working in us. The experience of 'Christ in me' becomes the experience of the Holy Spirit.

From the second sentence of the Spirit verse of the Trinity epistle, all statements about the healing Spirit are formulated in the subjunctive:

> *Grasping the Spirit through our humanity, we feel the*
>   *healing God.*
> *May he shine through the world as Spirit-light.*
> *May he shine in all that we behold.*
> *Our beholding be drenched with his Spirit-light.*

These statements of supplication express a longing for something that can only take place through human beings. The use of the subjunctive here can remind us of the Latin root of the word 'subjunctive': *to join*. In that sense, these subjunctive phrases call for the contact and mutual enhancement between the human soul and the Holy Spirit. As Thomas Aquinas put it so concisely, 'We can open our hearts to God, but only with divine help'.[1] There is no spiritual experience without participation. The epistle invites us to be active ourselves, but also leaves us completely free in this.

The first verse of the epistle, the Father verse, renews the original human being and, in the Christmas mood, presents us with the image of the primal, God-created human being. The Son verse gives us the ability to share in the death-conquering power of Christ. In the Easter mood, the new Adam – united with Christ – can arise in us, allowing us to participate in Christ's life, which he wrested from death. Then, in the Spirit verse, we experience the Pentecostal dimension of human greatness ('Grasping ... through our humanity') as well as of the individual human spirit. In grasping the Spirit, we simultaneously grasp our own innermost mission, yet this spiritual activity ('grasping') can only arise out of the spirit self of the individual. When it does, the I becomes bonded with humanity.

In this verse, we find a tension between the future yet to come and the present already dawning. The Pentecostal spiritual event has entered archetypally into humanity, and yet Pentecost always withdraws into the future – we cannot hold on to or control the spirit. Spirit is grace. Our being, gifted with spirit and entering into the spiritual community of the hierarchies who are burning in love, is illuminated in the Trinity epistle. As Paul puts it in his Letter to the Romans, 'Be aflame in Spirit' (12:11 literal translation). We can imagine this fire as a flame that joins with the other flames, forming a new community out of free individualities – through Christ who lives in us and between us.

> *May he graciously receive our knowing into his life*
>   *shining with spirit.*
> *May he fill with spirit all the ways of our human soul.*

3. TRINITY: THE TRINITARIAN HUMAN BEING

The epistle reveals to us our true nature, and each time we experience this, it is as if we are recreated anew.

- Spiritually behind me and protecting me, I experience the sustaining forces of the Father: I am born of him; he carries me.
- Spiritually at my side and accompanying me, I experience the Son's power to overcome death: I will live in him, even when I die.
- Spiritually in front of me and inspiring me from the future, I experience the healing power of the Spirit: in grasping this power, I myself create my eternity.

The Trinity epistle encompasses the divine as a whole. In the course of the year, it is our divine basis, serving as the house to which we return after the great festivals; the spiritual keynote of our world, from which the movements of the festivals arise. Depending on our openness to the spirit, we can – through the gateway of the epistle – participate in that which is already real in humanity through the forces of the Risen One.

4. Advent

Set Forth, Become Light

Advent is a spiritual New Year, when a new cycle of festivals begins. It is the time for deepening our inner Christian life. We see repetition in the festival cycle on a yearly basis, but we can picture it more as a spiral than a circle, for every festival can be seen as an octave of the previous year's festival – spiritually refreshed, inwardly more fulfilled and outwardly more effective. In this way, Christian festivals can gradually, year by year, transform our lives.

'Behold, I make all things new' (Rv 21:5). That is the ideal against which we must measure ourselves. If we ask ourselves 'Are we Christians yet?' the honest answer is probably 'no', but we are on the path of becoming Christian, and the festivals act as beacons on our journey. Christ became human so that we could become Christians and thus become fully human. The cycle of Christian festivals helps to transform us into Christians. It is a great, year-long Act of Consecration: as on a growing tree, a new growth-ring of our process of becoming Christian evolves from Advent to Advent.

Every new beginning of the inner year presents us with the task of approaching Christmas and Epiphany anew; then the next group of festivals, which includes Passiontide, Easter and Ascension; and finally, the three great festivals that resound like timpani drums through the festive year: Pentecost, St John's, and Michaelmas. The epistles of the Consecration of the Human Being allow us to experience the meaning of all these festivals in a completely new way.

4. ADVENT: SET FORTH, BECOME LIGHT

The Epistle of Advent expresses and fulfils our request expressed in the words, 'The Father God be in us.'

This petition to the divine Father that he may permeate us completely, that we may consciously experience his being within us, can be understood as a great, invisible headline for the whole Advent season, leading us into the origins of creation that emerged from the Father. It is a very special world into which we can immerse ourselves during Advent, full of poetic cadences and completely new yet mythical images:

> *Divine Might of Worlds,*
> *You who gleam in the chariot of the sun*
> *You who shine in the bow of colour*
> *Spanning the sky:*

We are introduced here to the mysteries of light and rainbows. Deep amazement emanates from the epistle, and it can also create this mood within us. It can engender in us a way of experiencing the world that is childlike in the best sense of the word – as a modern myth, or as a dream.

In the northern hemisphere, we experience the sun at this time of year more directly than in the summer months. It rises later and later, and we can 'practise' a little Advent by waiting for it every day. In asking ourselves new questions, we can connect with the course of the sun and learn to see it more intimately. What is the sunlight like in Advent? What sensations does it awaken in us? We can then gradually realise how the light at this time is quieter, more intimate, more restrained, even delicate. The sun itself seems to be more connected to its surroundings: the centre of a sea of colour. Think of the great Advent skies, conjured up in delicate, light pastel colours! Due to the low arc of the sun, we have a long dawn and dusk, the twilight periods in which day and night briefly join hands. Painters like Philipp Otto Runge, Caspar David Friedrich or William Turner had a special sense for these moods. In their works, the mysteries of transition appear as quiet, intimate colour festivals, woven from light and darkness.

The way the speech of the Advent epistle rhythmically breathes, opens up the interior of the outside world. The epistle begins with the motif of our souls opening up and beginning to perceive.

> *Our souls become deeply musing*
> *As we stand before the altar;*

What do our souls open up to? Advent literally means the arrival, the drawing near, the approach of what lies in the future; however, this does not happen by itself. It requires my attention, my being awake to what already exists, but is perhaps hidden. With regard to what has already taken place, we make a fine linguistic distinction in our experience of time. We either say this is 'past', in which case we no longer experience any real connection between the past and the present; or we can speak of 'what has been'. Saying, 'he has been there' has a different nuance: the way that his essence has connected with the situation or with the place has left traces and is still palpable or tangible in the present moment.

With regard to the future, we can also become more sensitive in our perception and make linguistic differentiations. We can speak of the future in the sense of 'sometime', completely vague as to *when* it will be, or even *if* it will happen at all – the 'unknown future'. However, there is also something coming from the future that is already making itself felt, something that is approaching, whose light already shines into the present, like dawn foretelling the sunrise. Although it has not yet arrived, it is already somehow present in its approaching – 'advent'. Corresponding to the 'has been', where something in the past still resonates in the present, one could speak of a foreshadowing, namely a hint of something existing in the future; an intimation of the future that becomes perceptible in the present. We are familiar with this in everyday life in witnessing an oncoming storm: we feel a closeness in the air and wait for the first flash of lightning. In many other situations, something announces itself in various foreshadowings, but we are often asleep to them and end up missing both the signs of what will be and what has been.

4. ADVENT: SET FORTH, BECOME LIGHT

Advent is the time to wake up to these signs, to become sensitive not only to everything that is coming, but also to develop the ability to perceive the arrival itself. We can develop two wings to our inner experience of time: the feeling for the essential in what has been, which we can call a sense for the echoes, and on the other hand, a feeling for what is essential in the future, which we can call a sense for foreshadowing. Only by developing these two 'wings of time' does our soul expand and become capable of the present, for this is how we can cultivate the conscious expectation of what is to come, the ability to rise to meet it, and the wish to receive it.

In this way, we touch the heart of a living Advent consciousness, for this means developing the power of anticipating the coming Christ. We learn in every moment to calmly stretch these wings of the soul in order to listen to what has been; from everything we experience, we learn to extract what is eternal, like a seed for the future, and thus, also to worthily receive what is coming towards us. In this way, the soul becomes capable of sensing time.

The parable of the ten virgins (Mt 25) tells of how only five of them can light their lamps. They have oil to feed the flame of attention, the flame of devotion to the future. The gates of their souls are open: they have prepared themselves to meet the bridegroom. The traditional Jewish custom in which the bride and groom are brought together serves here as an image of the human soul for the coming of Christ, for just as he came to humankind in physical form two thousand years ago, so today he is wanting to return anew in our consciousness.

'Arise, shine, for your light has come' (Is 60:1). Those who become light and shining are forming the soul into an organ for the true light that is to come into the world. Advent is the attunement to this. The Advent epistle trains our soul's openness to the future in order to receive the Christ worthily and to meet him in the sacred time of the Christmas season.

The motif of 'becoming' is the key to the entire Advent epistle. During Advent, the speaking of 'Divine Might of Worlds':

> *Is future word that softly*
> *Carries into the present.*
> *A 'Become' it speaks*

With *becoming* as the core of this epistle, Advent spurs us into a new cycle of growth at the beginning of our Christian year. Fuelling human development is at the core of what the cycle of Christian festivals, renewed in the ritual life of The Christian Community, offers us today. The festivals portray for us that through Christ a new creative power has entered into our dying and self-destructive world, into both earth and humanity. This 'future word' – *become* – is a message that comes to us from the future and which contains our own future within itself, for we are destined to become the image of God. A holy terror can pass through us when we hear the words of Christ in this sense, which John handed down to us: 'You are gods' (Jn 10:34, Ps 82:6). For at the same time, we are made 'out of the crooked timber of humanity' according to Kant,[1] or as Paul wrote, we want what is good – and yet we do evil (Rom 7:19).

It is precisely this tension between divine likeness and the threatening state of our world today that shows us most clearly the abyss of our freedom. We have freed ourselves from shackles and ties, but *for what* do we want to use our freedom?

Hannah Arendt wrote about freedom consisting of so much more than simply freeing ourselves from what binds us. The deep, unconscious question posed to us is whether we can make an inner experience of Christ the true content of our freedom. As Son of Man, he models for us what the human being can be when spiritually, mentally and physically permeated by the divine. In his book, *Hyperion,* Hölderlin wrote that 'Man is but a God when he becomes man'. In almost every line of the Advent epistle, processes of becoming are addressed. It leads us into a new becoming out of our narrow-mindedness or fixed ideas, out of our frenetic standstill where everything changes faster and faster but real change is not possible.

Goethe once said that to see someone as they are, makes them worse than they are, whereas seeing them as being in a process of

4. ADVENT: SET FORTH, BECOME LIGHT

becoming, raises them to their higher possibilities for the future, making them better. The 'become' that we hear in this epistle is an invitation to us, but at the same time a promise, a liberation into the future that says, 'You can leave the old behind you and set out for new shores.'

We hear this in the Gospel of John, when Christ tells the sick man at the pool of Bethesda, 'Get up! Pick up your mat and walk' (Jn 5:8). Christ's healing power does not work from without, but from within: he awakens in the man the courage to become. He gives him the strength to take up and truly own everything from the past that has been stored away.

An old mystery word is hidden in the future-oriented word 'become': *know yourself*. 'Become' is a metamorphosis of this ancient maxim. Through Christ, true self-knowledge leads to self-development or inner growth. The God of becoming helps us tap into this potential 'added value' that is hidden in every human being. 'The finished man, you know, is difficult to please; a growing mind will ever show you gratitude' (Goethe, *Faust I*, Prelude at the Theatre). Christ awakens these inner possibilities in us and rebuilds the archetype of the future human being.

> *A 'Become' it speaks*
> *And divining it awakens*
> *The picture of human becoming*

Friedrich Hebbel knew that the 'image of man' is associated with a great mystery. In truth, it is not about the image we form of the human being, but about the image that lives hidden within us, which will one day become a future reality. The 'image of man' is thus the future within us – our becoming and our goal as human beings.

> Have respect for the image of man,
> And think that within it lies, however hidden,
> For some future tomorrow, a seed
> That wants to grow to the heights.

> Have respect for the image of man,
> And think that, however deep it lies,
> There can spring from your soul
> An awakening breath of life!²

In the following, the Advent epistle reveals to us an even deeper mystery that is also connected with becoming human, namely, that in our becoming human, God, too, is 'becoming'.

> *And divining it awakens*
> *The picture of human becoming*
> *In which God's becoming lies hidden.*

'God's becoming' – what a statement! We usually think of God as perfect, eternal, even unchanging. Even though everything in the world is in a state of change, religion tells us there is an eternal ground of the world, an axis that supports and holds everything and is itself unchanging. Yet now this divine ground of being itself is spoken of as a becoming? How are we to imagine this? Philosophers and theologians have long puzzled over this. If God is thought of as changeable, then it can only mean a change for the better, but that presupposes that God is not yet perfect. A God undergoing a growing process seems to contradict all conventional theology.

In his essay 'The Concept of God after Auschwitz', Hans Jonas explored his thoughts on the question of how God can be conceived as one becoming.³ Being Jewish, Jonas outlines how the Jewish God is also a God of history: Judaism is strongly oriented to the history of the Jewish people, from the calling of Abraham to the expectation of the Messiah. This sense of history and of being since the beginning of time the 'chosen people' makes what happened to the Jewish people in the twentieth century incomprehensible. Where was God? Why did he not prevent the Holocaust? Jonas finds an answer in the idea of freedom: God wants people to be free, which is why he voluntarily withdrew his divine omnipotence, limiting his own power in order to give human beings

4. ADVENT: SET FORTH, BECOME LIGHT

the freedom and capability to develop their individuality. God has long since refrained from intervening directly in the fate of humanity, which is why the question, 'How could God allow all this?' is misguided. God believes in free human beings.

On the other hand, writes Jonas, God is by no means indifferent to all that happens on earth and to people. He is and remains God in history. He experiences, feels and suffers with what people on earth think, speak and do, and this engagement changes him – simply because every experience by definition effects change! God himself is in the process of becoming by virtue of living through all that humanity undergoes.

From the perspective of Christianity, we can add that through Christ becoming human and entering into the history of humanity, God himself is undergoing our deeds and our suffering – and thus, becoming – together *with* us.

The Advent epistle testifies to the risk of God's radical love for humanity. It speaks of the active grace that lives in God's heart, which wants to integrate all the error that flows from us into his own divine soul and transform it there, as depicted in the parable of the prodigal son. Ultimately, the 'lost' son is welcomed and even celebrated by the loving father who had never stopped waiting for his son to return. Forgiving love is found in the becoming of God:

> *God's becoming, which in grace*
> *Would shelter and redeem*
> *Our errors, full of mercy*
> *In his own divine soul.*

The Act of Consecration in Advent, with the blue of the vestments and the tree next to the altar that awakens a memory of paradise, expands our soul, stretches it and fills it with awe. It brings to mind Mary's Magnificat at the beginning of the Gospel of Luke (1:46), 'My soul magnifies the Lord.' While most translations use the word 'magnifies' it could also be translated as 'My soul *grows great* in praising you, O Lord'. Our expanding soul becomes Mary-like, tuned to Advent, like an instrument prepared to make music. The epistle then leads our soul, thus attuned, on a path. In the blue colour of the Advent service, adults are invited to experience inwardly what children experience in the Advent garden: the inner light is ignited when the soul walks the spiral leading inwards. Our soul becomes a large sensory organ for what is to come, so that our eyes are opened. Ancient depictions show us high angelic beings whose bodies and wings are covered with eyes.

Feeling inwardly upright while participating in the Act of Consecration of the Human Being awakens a priestly quality in the human soul. Our soul senses the reality of the spirit that it faces, and, in this way, the service becomes an intimation of the spirit. Silence enters, becomes more perceptible, then palpable. In silence, we can become fully attentive! It awakens our organs of hearing, which convey deep impressions to us. We listen into the inaudible, and the silence itself begins to speak. We are rediscovering that this spirit word is ringing through our world, that the divine speaks to us in the gleaming of the chariot of the sun, and in the shining of the bow of colour. That which is of the heavenly realm seems to want to approach us.

Two thousand years ago, the womb of the world received new life – the maternal aspect that serves as the fundament of our world welcomed the Redeemer of humankind: the Saviour, the bringer of salvation for all peoples and for the maltreated natural world. For each individual to realise the truth of this fact requires conscious preparation, like the gardener preparing the soil, so that the seed of salvation can successfully grow in our hearts:

> *Our heart can sense*
> *The salvation that in the womb of worlds*
> *Quickens in promise,*
> *That in the inmost soul*
> *Of the mysteries of the world,*
> *Comforting human beings,*

4. ADVENT: SET FORTH, BECOME LIGHT

Prophetic in dark world night,
Speaks, announcing its work
In the realm of earth.[4]

Consolation emanates from this experience of intimation, creating trust in the great 'nevertheless'. This assurance lifts us up in the Advent light that streams towards us:

Working in the realm of earth,
That speaks prophetically
In the gleaming of the chariot of the sun
In the shining of the bow of colour
That spans the sky.

We hear about the purification and preparation of the heart throughout the Advent epistle, intimately tender and at the same time cosmically powerful, building the manger for the birth of Christ.

The Advent epistle awakens us both to the mysteries of Advent visible in the cosmic phenomena and to the subtle inner perceptions in the depths of our soul. There, the inner listening begins to perceive the audible reign of the Father-Ground of being. The world in its depths begins to speak to us in a similar way as a piece of art that we are contemplating, where we feel an encounter – or even a reciprocal relationship – taking place. This inner dialogue gives rise to the call, 'Become! For you are not yet truly human. Seek your path of becoming human.'

Look in the eye those powers that want to divert you from this path by dragging you down into despair, saying, 'You worm, all your ideals are only illusions; you are weak and will always remain so.' Also look the powers in the eye that want to deceive you by saying, 'You are already perfect, you just have to discover it in yourself. You don't need any painstaking development – you are already divine.' Both these powers stand in the way of your becoming human; both try to prevent it. There, between despair and arrogance, the door to Advent opens, offering the grace of *becoming.* Defying the temptations of despair allows us to overcome the darkness and gives us hope again, while separating ourselves from the impulses of pride makes us humble.

The central gospel of the Advent season (Lk 21) is taken from a depiction of what took place on Maundy Thursday. Oppressed and attacked, Christ knows he is nearing his death. He is filled with the intention to fulfil his mission on earth and does so in the deepest humility, saying, 'Your will be done ...' In this situation he sketches a view of the future for the disciples to prepare them for the world's Advent:

> There will be signs in the sun, moon and stars. On the earth, nations will be in anguish and perplexity at the roaring and tossing of the sea. People will faint from terror, apprehensive of what is coming on the world, for the heavenly bodies will be shaken. (Lk 21:25f)

This imaginative-dramatic preview ultimately enters a space of cosmic calm, like the eye of a storm: 'At that time they will see the Son of Man coming in a cloud with power and great glory' (Lk 21:27). Advent in the cosmos – Advent in the soul!

The Advent gospel reading ends with instructions for the human soul regarding how it can, as a bride-to-be, stand upright before the coming Son of Man, her Bridegroom, the Saviour.

Through the Advent epistle, new light is shed upon the end of the Creed, which follows the Gospel Reading. Insofar as Advent makes heaven and earth appear in a new light, it gives new colour and brilliance to the first sentence of the Creed, which speaks of 'an almighty divine being, spiritual-physical' being 'the ground of existence of the heavens and the earth'. Everything enters into a new becoming through Christ sent by the Father.

By connecting and allying ourselves with Christ, the perspective of a cosmic Advent also opens up for us at the end of the Creed, enveloping us in a mood of hope beyond all abysses and downfalls: 'They may hope for the overcoming of the sickness of sin; for the preservation of man's being; and for the preservation of their life, destined for eternity.'

The Creed is harmoniously followed by the Advent inserted prayer, which speaks of the coming salvation. Firstly, we are taken into the experience of cosmic twilight. The northern hemisphere lends itself well to this experience, for the winter months here are the twilight of the year. A dramatic change is hidden in the stillness of twilight. Something fades away and loses itself in the distance, for something new is dawning. Something emerges from the darkness of our consciousness:

Divining grows from twilight

We sense that creation itself is not a finished product but a living process, that the world seems to emerge anew every morning from the primal ground of existence, and that in Advent, the processes of decaying, disappearing and new becoming all join hands in the invisible. The Advent inserted prayer after the Creed leads us into the interior of this process. The essence of the Word is working behind and in all natural events: the heart of nature, indeed of the world, is the creative and formative Word: 'The world was made through him' (Jn 1:10).

The creative cosmic Word enters the world anew in Advent to renew and revitalise creation – it seeks to reconnect human beings, who have arisen out of the Word, with their origin. By beginning to feel this in our soul, we can tune into the Advent hymn, which in turn attunes us to the coming of the holy Word of the creator, to the incarnation of the Logos:

> *Hail to our divining*
> *Hail to our hoping,*
> *Hail to the light-born*
> *Hail to the colour-carried*
> *Eternal, divine-wielding*
> > *Word.*

Explanatory notes

The ritual colour in Advent is blue. It appears on the antependium of the altar and on the vestments. Blue expands our souls. The archetype of this colour is the sky, which is blue because the colour arises when turbidity is illuminated in front of darkness.

In the early summer of 1924, Rudolf Steiner described yet another aspect of the colour blue. Blue is a borderline perception, in that it appears at the end or the beginning of the etheric at the boundary to the physical:

> If you were to look, so to speak, at ... ether, you see nothing with your physical senses, you would simply see through it. The ether seems invisible or non-existent.
> But when you regard the whole etheric environment, you behold the blue sky, which is also not really there. Yet it appears blue because you are actually perceiving the end of the ether ... When we see the blue sky, we are in fact really perceiving the ether around us.

By immersing ourselves in the blue, we learn to move and live in the etheric. We gradually develop our own luminosity in the etheric, so that Christ can appear in the light that we stream towards him etherically in openness and devotion. Becoming one with the blue could be seen as an 'ascension experience':

> To our immediate vision the ether remains imperceptible, yet it allows itself to become visible in the blue heavens. The right way for us to express our perception of the blue of the sky is to say, 'We cannot see the ether, but it rises before our vision, becoming perceptible, through the greatness and majesty with which it spreads out through the universe, revealing itself in the heavens' blue expanse.'[5]

4. ADVENT: SET FORTH, BECOME LIGHT

We encounter the image of the sun chariot in Greek mythology. Helios, the sun god, drives the chariot into the morning sky and illuminates the day. We find it mentioned in Euripides' drama *Ion*, written around 412 BC. These are the first lines of the initial monologue of Ion ('the walking one', the son of Creusa and Apollo):

> Now flames this radiant chariot of the sun
> High o'er the earth, at whose ethereal fire
> The stars into the sacred night retreat:
> O'er the Parnassian cliffs the ascending wheels
> To mortals roll the beams of day.[6]

By contrast, in the Advent epistle we hear about the chariot of the sun as a *prophetic* image, for it is the divine world power of salvation that speaks: 'You who gleam in the chariot of the sun.' In this way, we hear echoes of the cosmic Advent of pre-Christian cultures repeated, making it possible for every participant to experience the grandeur of the salvation event. As Mary cried out in praise in her Magnificat, 'my soul grows great …'

Clement of Alexandria (*c.* 145–220) relates the image of Helios with the chariot of the sun directly to Christ, calling him 'the Sun of Righteousness who drives his chariot over all':

> For in us, buried, in darkness, shut up in the shadow of death, light has shone forth from heaven, purer than the sun, sweeter than life here below. That light is eternal life; and whatever partakes of it lives … For 'the Sun of Righteousness', who drives his chariot over all, pervades equally all humanity, like 'his Father, who makes his sun to rise on all men', and distils on them the dew of the truth.[7]

The image of the victorious Helios rushing through the sky in his shining chariot becomes the 'triumphal chariot' of the resurrection, to which the 'gleam' of the chariot in the Advent epistle prophetically points. The word 'triumphal' here is a reference to this apt description by a fourth-century Roman known as Julius Firmicus Maternus:

> Lo, after three days the day rises brighter than is its wont, the sun regains the glory of its quondam luster, and Christ almighty God is adorned with the rays of a more resplendent sun. The Godhead of Salvation exults, and the throng of the just and the saints attends his triumphal chariot.[8]

Finally, Zeno of Verona (300–371) associates the image of the sun chariot with the solar year, which symbolises the divine power of the world with the four seasons:

> The day of salvation has come to the driver of the eternal chariot, who orients his pathway around the final destination in an annual cycle. He follows himself, he precedes himself; he is old and yet always young: procreator of the year and offspring of the year. (*Tractatus* II, 49)

Through these examples, we can trace a feeling among early Christians for the chariot of the sun being a vessel for the Christ.

The 'bow of colour that spans the sky' initially reminds us of God's covenant with humankind, which is associated with the sign of the rainbow:

> I have set my rainbow in the clouds, and it will be the sign of the covenant between me and the earth. Whenever I bring clouds over the earth and the rainbow appears in the clouds, I will remember my covenant between me and you and all living creatures of every kind. (Gen 9:13–15)

Interestingly, the rainbow is described below as a memory that God gives himself, which he looks at 'from above':

4. ADVENT: SET FORTH, BECOME LIGHT

> Whenever the rainbow appears in the clouds, I will see it
> and remember the everlasting covenant between God and
> all living creatures of every kind on the earth. (Gen 9:16)

The rainbow appears again in the throne vision of Ezekiel in 597 BC. Ezekiel was a priest in Jerusalem who was deported to Babylon when the Babylonians conquered Jerusalem.[9] He had a prophetic vision of a throne above the firmament, in the blue of heaven: '... high above on the throne was a figure like that of a man' (Ezk 1:26). Ezekiel sees the highest divinity in the image of the human being, whose glory appears around him like an arc of colour:

> I saw that from what appeared to be his waist up he looked
> like glowing metal, as if full of fire, and that from there
> down he looked like fire; and brilliant light surrounded
> him. Like the appearance of a rainbow in the clouds on
> a rainy day, so was the radiance around him. This was
> the appearance of the likeness of the glory of the LORD.
> (Ezk 1:27f)

The divine Son has clothed himself in the archetype of the human being. Putting on the archetype like a robe, he appears as a human being, as *the* human being. A divine glory surrounds him, appearing as the heavenly arc of colours, for which the earthly rainbow is an image. Wrapped in the garment of this rainbow, Jesus Christ makes the covenant of God become human. The Greek myth of the chariot of the sun and the ancient Hebrew prophecy of the Son of Man in the splendour of the colours unite in the renewed experience of Advent. We await the salvation 'that speaks with promise in the hoping human heart ... in the chariot of the sun in the bow of colour spanning the sky'.

Speaking to members of the School of Spiritual Science, Rudolf Steiner expounded on the image of the rainbow in a grandiose way, calling it a 'mighty imagination'. The rainbow is not just a symbol of the Old Testament covenant of the Godhead with the people of Israel, but a gift for us that we can understand as a symbol pointing to the future. For today's spiritual disciple, it represents the gateway to the spiritual world. The Guardian of the Threshold points the individual to this powerful imagination, which, if he has the eyes to see it, can be perceived as something tremendously majestic. He can learn to feel how the spiritual world shines in through the colourful glow of the rainbow. The memory of the image of the rainbow creates the connection between the spiritual and physical world. The power of seeing can be transformed in order to enter the real spiritual world through the 'bow of colour'.

Seen through the inner gaze, the arc of colours becomes an immense chalice, the colours flooding and flowing through one another. Steiner describes how through this 'ether-rainbow', the work of the hierarchies opens up in the world vessel's colour-flooding light, transforming and substantiating all that is earthly.

When the power of the imagination is withdrawn, room is made for the *inner* Word – the Word that speaks from the depths of the spiritual disciple who is filled with the longing for the living, divine Word: 'I will to feel the Being of Christ.'[10]

This is expressed in the Advent inserted prayer.

> *Hail to our divining*
> *Hail to our hoping,*
> *Hail to the light-born*
> *Hail to the colour-carried*
> *Eternal, divine-wielding*
> *   Word.*

Jörg Ewertowski has posed the question of the becoming of God in a new way, namely in the context of an anthroposophical understanding of evolution. While the medieval stance was that the perfection of God precludes any change, in the modern era, the idea of development has come to the fore with the argument that if God himself does not develop, he lacks the ability

4. ADVENT: SET FORTH, BECOME LIGHT

to develop. This corresponds to the specifically modern idea of infinite development.

The source of all future development is the Mystery of Golgotha, for it is in that event that the end and the beginning converge, forming a new centre: the centre of time. As Ewertowski put it, 'The end of the death on the cross and the beginning of the resurrection not only mark the centre of earthly development ... but the centre of *all* development.'[11]

The human I was actually born only in this midpoint of time, and with it, the principle of human becoming. The I is the principle of the transformation of the different parts of the human being, and hidden inside the I is the divine: 'The God who dwells within the human being begins to speak when the soul recognises itself as an I.'[12]

The Advent epistle echoes the fact that this transformation is at the same time linked to the re-establishment and fulfilment of the image of the human being. It speaks of becoming human, a mysterious process that somehow also harbours God's becoming.

In this context, I think it is worth mentioning an extraordinary statement by John Scotus Eriugena from the ninth century, which Martin Buber used as the motto for *Daniel: Dialogues on Realisation,* an early prose work: *Deus in creatura mirabili et ineffabili modo creatur* – God is created in his creatures in a wondrous and ineffable way.

The Trinity harbours as an innermost mystery the origin of God's becoming, for the Trinity is the fountainhead of time itself. The Logos emerges from eternity as the Son, which is how time came into being, and with it, the activity of becoming. The Logos became the 'Son born in eternity'. His creative power permeates Christ, the lofty being of the Sun. We can hardly grasp in our soul – let alone our intellect – how this supreme power of the Logos passes step by step through the hierarchies down into the earthly world. We can say Christ died from the sun towards the earth. This had become necessary because not only the earth, but – and this is hardly conceivable – the supersensible world itself had reached an end. Rudolf Steiner wrote: 'Death, after all, merely expresses the fact that the supersensible world had previously reached a point beyond which it could not advance by its own efforts.'

The sense world has become fertile ground for a higher world! The spiritual world needed to pass through the sensory world that Jesus Christ accomplished through his death and resurrection. As a result, the human being has become the growing point for the advancement of the world, as it is stated in the Creed. 'Indeed, only if certain beings evolved with the appropriate faculties in the physical realm could the supersensible realm advance in evolution.'[13]

Christ's incarnation and overcoming of death have formed for humanity the basis for freedom and love, which we may continue to develop as faculties. These capacities will in turn become the seeds for the advancement of the world, insofar as human becoming unites with divine becoming.

5. Christmas

Christ of All the Earth

There is such a contrast between the unavoidably busy quality of the weeks leading up to Christmas and the midnight church service. A particular silence and mood of mystery belong to midnight, a time when most people are usually asleep. The room is alive with a level of concentration, seriousness and expectation that can feel unfamiliar for some people at first. The midnight Christmas service invites us to immerse ourselves in the archetypal events – we are allowed to participate in the renewed mysteries. Until the bright light of day, we go through three stages, which already existed in the pre-Christian mysteries. Imbued with the mystery of Christ, we now experience them anew: preparation (*catharsis*), enlightenment (*photismos*) and fulfilment (*teleiōsis*).

Christmas Eve is a silent, deep preparation. December 24 was traditionally called Adam and Eve Day, from which we can infer that Christmas can only be understood through its relationship to the mysteries of paradise. The myth of Adam and Eve presents us an image of the fate of humankind: God-created human beings who cannot resist seduction by adversarial powers, who turn away from God and must now find their way on earth outside of paradise. The whole concern of the divine world is that this earthly path not be our undoing. We are faced with the question of whether we will combine the freedom given to us prematurely by adversarial powers with our love and loyalty to the divine world of our origin. Will the apostate ever want to turn to God again? Will we recognise and open ourselves to the grace of Christmas?

Three masses are celebrated at Christmas in the Roman Catholic Church, too, the names of which carry an air of solemnity: *in nocte, in aurora,* and *in die,* meaning at midnight, at dawn, and in broad daylight. These three sacraments form a whole; we can think of them as one great service.

At midnight we raise ourselves to the silent expanses of the cosmos to receive Christ's light of grace. The love of Christ for the earth is rekindled.

In the second service, his light, which permeates the darkness of the earth, begins to come alive in our souls in the early dawn. In remembering the warmth of the shepherds, whose devotion and piety are archetypes of an inner prayerful mood, our own heart-sensitivity and warmth flow towards the divine child. We recognise in the newborn the Logos, the divine cosmic Word, drawing near to humanity. We ask that this cosmic Word suffuse us, warm us, and empower us.

In the third service, in the bright light of day, the bud of the Christmas event can truly blossom, filling our waking consciousness with heartfelt clarity. The intimate feeling we cultivated in the preceding services is joined by bright and generously outpouring Christmas thinking.

Christmas! What a multitude of facets we associate with this word; vivid memories from childhood come flooding back to us. Christmas is the festival of light, the festival of light in the darkness. We can sense a spiritual light in the Christmas lights, as if they are touched by a higher splendour, a 'magic from above'. The light of knowing is a basic motif in the Christmas Acts of Consecration: in all three Christmas services, we hear the following words:

> *Know this:*
> *Christ has appeared in the realm of earth*

This initiation-like character of Christianity – the way it guides us on a path towards deeper knowledge – is revealed in this holy night, especially in the three Christmas services.[1] In

5. CHRISTMAS: CHRIST OF ALL THE EARTH

the midnight Consecration of the Human Being, we consciously enter the darkness like initiates. As preparation for initiation in the ancient mysteries, the candidates would sit in silence for hours in the darkness. The soul could awaken to the darkness, and in confronting the dark, become light, so that when it suddenly became light, the bright light was not just perceived, but known and recognised as profound reality. Christmas is the night in which new light shines into the earthly world. (The German word Christmas, *Weihnachten,* literally means 'night of consecration'.) The light shone *into* the darkness, and since then it has continued to shine *within* the darkness.

The original source of light for us is the sun. Without its light, its power and its life, we cannot exist. The physical sun is, however, also an image of Christ. The Gospel describes the transfiguration of Christ on the mountain: how his nature bursts forth from Jesus like the radiant sun after a thunderstorm. 'His face shone like the sun, and his clothes became as white as the light' (Mt 17:2). Christ is the spiritual sun being, and our physically visible sun indicates the direction in which we can seek the nature of Christ, according to a true inner vision. In the Christmas Children's Service, this being is described to them as 'Christ, the brightly shining Spirit Sun'. From the children's perspective, the visible sun and the spiritual sun are still one, which can be often seen in their drawings of the sun with a face.

As adults, we are initially deprived of this way of seeing it. We are completely immersed in the sensory world and have adopted a narrow field of vision that leaves no room for the child's imaginative perception. Christmas can, however, raise questions that concern us all. Is the sensory world everything? Where has that Christmas magic of our childhood gone? Was it just an illusion? Is there a way to return to a genuine Christmas experience as an adult?

The epistle in the midnight service looks at our earthly world from out of the spirit.[2] It is night on earth, and darkness envelops our senses, both internally and externally: we have lost the spiritual and must seek it anew. Our own deepest being cannot be found in the sensory world. The midnight epistle addresses this situation by offering us both diagnosis and therapy at the same time, announcing how a new light shines into the night of materialism, into a humanity far from God: the light of grace.

Into earth-night
Into sense-darkness
Streams the Spirit's
Healing light of grace

It shines on all people and on the earth as a whole, but can only become effective in us when we, be it out of joy or out of need, lift ourselves up to the divine world. All sorts of births belong to today's Christmas – also those that arise out of despair, longing, or crises. New ways of celebrating these births can be created where the old ones are no longer relevant, as long as one keeps in mind the decisive factor of the spiritual background of all Christmas celebrations: recognising for ourselves that the healing light of grace shines through Christ on this night and that a ray of this light reaches every person.

Do we feel this in the depths of our prayer?

Christmas is the time of year when a childlike mood of prayer returns to us, spurring us on to give thanks, to feel accepted, and to joyfully embrace our life. We begin to sense that we are loved. This is the beginning of a new prayer.

Into earth-night
Into sense-darkness
Streams the Spirit's
Healing light of grace
It streams forth to us
When we walk
Freed from the body in the land of spirits
After the heart within us
Has felt it in divining prayer.

5. CHRISTMAS: CHRIST OF ALL THE EARTH

What we experience in the midnight service – cosmically vast and characterised by deep mystery – in the dawn service appears quite close to our heart. While we hear the beginning of the Gospel of Matthew at midnight – and thus the beginning of the four gospels and the bridge from the Old to the New Testament – at dawn, we immerse ourselves in the pastoral mood. The gospel leads us with the shepherds to the manger to kneel in devotion before the child.

Just like the one in the midnight service, the epistle in the Christmas dawn service is only heard once a year – remarkable in an age when everything tends to be available at any place and at any time. This is part of what makes it a very special treasure, reminiscent of earlier times when special altarpieces were only made accessible during certain festivals. Embedded in the heart-warming mood of the shepherds, the epistle of the second Christmas service turns our attention to the Logos. The shepherds themselves already lived in the Logos, under the open, starlit sky. Their souls opened wide as they surrendered to the heavenly world, and they could feel the laws of the cosmos and the Logos.

Through the Christmas event, we can immerse ourselves in the shepherd-borne renewal of the Word. The Word is born anew every year at Christmas, and we may feel the 'healing Creator Word' draw near to us again. Are we prepared for this? Do we realise what this means for our speaking and listening through the whole of the coming year?

Fatherly Ground of the World:
Our soul feels the drawing near
Of the healing Creator-Word

In the epistle we ask for the blessing power of the Logos for our human word, so that the Word might live on our 'speaking lips'. We pray that when we speak, our words may come from the spiritual warmth of our hearts, and that from our mouth may flow what has come alive in our heart. Finally, we pray that the Word may seek us with its blessing in this hour; we ask for the strengthening of our will, so that his powers might pour through the spirit into the service of humanity and our earth. We ask that we may become true speakers through the blessing of the divine Word:

> *May his power stream to us in blessing,*
> *That he touch our speaking lips,*
> *And warm our speech-bearing blood*
> *And strengthen our spirit-devoted willing*
> *Through all future cycles of time.*

The third service takes place in broad daylight: Christmas morning has dawned, and we experience the Act of Consecration out of the same Christmas spirit but with its own unique character. With full daylight we experience a kind of contagious joy within and around us. Out of this mood of rejoicing, the epistle reveals deep truths that are hidden in the Christ-being and the Christ-event, which may now be proclaimed.

The third Christmas epistle speaks in a special way of the incarnation of Christ, the revealing creative spirit of the Father. We hear an old and solemn word used: *erkoren,* which, in English is translated as 'chosen'. In German it has a solemn but celebratory feeling to it, communicating the import of the preparation of Christ's earthly body. The 'body of the earth' is also quietly alluded to in the term 'earthly body'.

> *Christ, the revealing Creator-Spirit*
> *Of the Fatherly Ground of the World*
> *Has chosen the earthly body*
> *In which he would dwell.*

In Jesus we see the human being who has been prepared over generations to become the vessel for the Christ, giving him a home in pure selflessness. Thus the Christmas Service for Children speaks of 'the child Jesus, who became the Christ'. Jesus made himself more and more into a vessel for Christ, and thus Christ was able to become more and more human. We could therefore also think in terms of 'Christ who then became Jesus'; after all, he sacrifices his divine being in order to redeem the human being, to guide us back to our origin and allow us to blossom anew. Christ incarnated for this purpose – this is why he promised to stay by us humans, then and forever (Mt 28:20). We can experience this anew at Christmas. This is the spiritual core of Christmas joy and cheer: he has chosen the earthly body![3]

Christ truly became human in the full, bodily sense, which enabled him to counter the adversarial powers on earth. This is the essence of Christianity: Christ incarnated fully into the human body – just as at the end of his life on earth, he really did go through death in order to save us.

Why do we call Christ our Saviour? What does he save us from? According to the epistle, he saves us from the dominion of the opposing powers, the effects of which we carry within us as sickness and death, as a tendency towards selfishness, and as an inclination towards untruth. The depth of the Christmas story can only be grasped when we place Christ's act, his incarnation, between the opposing powers that threaten us and from which he can save us – if we want him to.

The fact that we need Christ is unequivocally stated in the epistle. We have strayed from becoming the human beings that the divine world had intended. We strayed – and continue to do so repeatedly – in two directions. We are in danger of falling prey on the one hand to the 'false light', and on the other hand, to 'unworthy craving'. These two formulations can become a beacon of knowledge for us, whose light can help us examine ourselves. Is the light I am chasing a divine, healing, warming light, or is it rather a deceptive, illusory light? Likewise, are my relations to the sensory world characterised by loving devotion? Do I seek joy and beauty in the sense world? Or do I relate to the world of senses rather out of a need to fill a hunger? Am I responding to addictive tendencies? The words 'false light' and 'unworthy craving' help us to recognise temptations.

This power of recognising and gradually defeating these adversarial forces, belongs to Christ. He became human in order to redeem us from these adversarial forces. Without understanding this earnest purpose, Christmas and all its celebrations become sentimental.

> *To save us*
> *From the deceiving false light,*
> *To save us*
> *From the senses' unworthy craving*
> *In all future cycles of time.*[4]

After the initial epistles at midnight, at dawn and in broad daylight, we now hear a call to *know*. The priest turns to the congregation and proclaims, 'Know this'. This is the keynote of the true modern Christmas celebration. At the core of Christmas lies a challenge to come to knowledge, which one can only accomplish on one's own. Christmas is a festival of knowing: without it, Christmas would not really be Christmas! True knowledge arises gradually: the light that the soul attains in and through the darkness is what allows us – step by step – to feel and recognise the mystery spoken of in the words, 'God is light' (1Jn 1:5). This light, born out of darkness, is the light that we carry into the sacrament, and is also the light that allows us to understand the cosmic mystery that the epistle of midnight reveals to us in these monumental words:

> *Into earth-night*
> *Into sense-darkness*
> *Streams the Spirit's*
> *Healing light of grace*

That which has separated us from the Godhead, our exodus from paradise, is lifted up. We look inwardly towards him, who again unlocks the gates to paradise. This gate opens through the seriousness of the night, through the mood of initiation that prepares our heart to create for itself a conscious Christmas experience. When the Christmas bells ring out, awakening deep joy, the

5. CHRISTMAS: CHRIST OF ALL THE EARTH

feeling heart and the clear, knowing consciousness ring together, echoing the bells. Prayer becomes a knowing, knowing becomes a holy prayer. Like soil in the spring, the soul is cultivated and prepared to receive the task of knowing, which will then lead it to find true freedom in divine freedom. We are to recognise that the Christ has appeared in the earthly kingdom. We are to see in him the saviour of the people of the earth – the one who has reopened the way to the divine Father, to the Ground of all Being.

The Christmas event as a turning point in time, as the beginning of a new era has inscribed itself on the earth to such an extent that it lights up as script above and on the altar during the Christmas festival season. It is the Christmas message to the shepherds that shines forth as if from the earth itself, as soon as we reignite the Christmas light. Our light makes visible again what has been invisibly spoken and inscribed on the earth ever since the choirs of angels sang their song on that first Christmas night:

> Revealed be God in the heights
> and on earth peace to all of good will.[5]

Above this appears in large letters: K M B or C M B. On the one hand, the sound of the letters embody the elemental forces of the cosmos. Behind the sound of K (or C) we can experience the work of the Cherubim from the realm of Sagittarius the Centaur. He is half human and half animal, but directs his will like an arrow towards the future, aiming at the future of becoming fully human. Behind the M-sound we sense the power of Aquarius, who is also depicted as an angelic being, showing us an image of our own future. With the M, we find the wisdom of 'middle', 'medium', and 'measure'. Behind the sound of B lives the power of Virgo the Virgin who forms the vessel for what is new and becoming. These three great cosmic signs present us with challenges: the K (or C) calls us to apply the strength of our will for the future, while keeping the 'measure and middle' of M, in order to build the B: the dwelling for the child within us.

On the other hand, these letters also represent the initials of Kaspar (or Caspar), Melchior and Balthasar, the three kings who enlivened the forces of the zodiac described above within themselves, thereby becoming images of the cosmic K M B or C M B in the human realm.[6]

This script remains visible as a backdrop throughout the Christmas period. What is otherwise hidden – and with the end of the Christmas season returns to obscurity – now shines out, full of grace, in golden letters. Nietzsche wrote in his book *Thus Spoke Zarathustra* (Ch. 40), 'The heart of the earth is of gold', and in that sense, we can imagine that a secret message of the earth has been inscribed using this gold: 'Christ of all the earth'.

The inserted prayer after the Offertory, which we only hear in the third service and for the remaining days of Christmas, is the crowning glory of the Christmas ritual. It is often called the Hymn to the Hierarchies due to its content. Although the choirs of angels certainly belong to the archetype of the child in the manger, it is only now in the daylight of the third sacrament that we invoke them. They become 'angels of the daytime' at Christmas: out of the holy night, they enter into our full daytime consciousness. The realm of the nine angelic hierarchies, from the angels to the Seraphim, is a present spiritual reality that spans the Christmas altar like a mighty rainbow. Only after the Offertory and out of the mood of offering is this sacred mystery revealed to us, for only then do we hear the names of these beings ring out; only then may we join in their eternal 'song of offering'.

The language of the inserted prayer is complex, structured according to the 'grammar of the Holy Spirit'. It begins by addressing God the Father, uniting the objective side of his being ('Ground of all Being') with the paternal side that faces towards us ('Fatherly'):

Fatherly Ground of all Being

5. CHRISTMAS: CHRIST OF ALL THE EARTH

He is the one we turn to; it is he to whom we speak. Then, step by step, a kind of Christmas pyramid is built up before us: each layer supporting the next. An inner heightening of the Christmas event is unveiled that allows us human beings to step up into the life and work of the angelic realms. The building of these steps begins with our understanding of the original Christmas event – the incarnation of Christ and his entire earthly life – as the basis of all that follows:

In that through the Word,
Who lived in the earthly body

The fact that the Word became flesh – *et incarnatus est* – is the heart of the Christmas event. How does it then become fruitful for the becoming of the world? That path is now shown to us. What is now expressed as fact, as the inner after-effect in human soul life, is surprising and even challenging:

In that through the Word,
Who lived in the earthly body ...
The light of your clear shining-power
Has disclosed itself
To our spiritual beholding

These two long lines are encompassed in an extended breath. By listening to them attentively, we create within ourselves an expansiveness for the Christmas stages of the soul that are being developed before us: the earthly life of the Logos communicates a bit of its light to our spiritual vision, and in so doing, dispels the darkness within us. This is the core of the Christmas celebration – to allow his 'clear shining-power' to shine within us.

The next stage builds on this. What do we want to use this gift of 'clear shining-power' for? In the following we are made aware of what the divine world intends in giving the Christmas light of Christ to every human being:

> *That we come to know the divine*
> *Through what is seen*

Christmas is the season for focussing on our process of knowing – it is a time to work on basing religion on new knowledge, so that we recognise that the Son of God has appeared in the visible man Jesus, but also learn to recognise that, since his sacrifice out of love, he lives in everything visible. Christmas is a time for empowering ourselves to see the divine in the visible again. This particular Christmas knowledge will come into being through the light of this new 'shining-power' given to us.

It does not stop here, however – another step on the ladder to heaven follows. Within the Christmas-renewed, childlike openness, a new pure love is kindled for all that is. We feel anew that the visible world is like a great transparent image. Beings who grace us make the material world light up and glow. The more we awaken to it and learn to recognise it with wonder, the more a quiet love for the divine grows within us. In the Christmas light we learn to see and recognise the world anew.

> *And thereby for the unseen our love be kindled*

By learning and practising the stages of the Christmas process of knowing, we become worthy of joining the work of the hierarchies. They are always there, carrying out the will of the divine, but reveal themselves to our consciousness only in the Christmas light. This is when humans and angels may come together, joining in song of praise and looking to the Fatherly Ground of all Being.

> *We join in the offering-song*
> *Of the Angels, Archangels, of the Archai,*
> *Of the Revealers, of the World Powers, of the World Guides,*
> *Of the Thrones, of the Cherubim and Seraphim*

5. CHRISTMAS: CHRIST OF ALL THE EARTH

We are allowed to join the angelic realms in their offering-song, as the epistle calls it. This song serves the ongoing revelation of God's being in people's souls, for whose salvation he himself became human. This sacred hymn has a deep meaning in world events, which we hear about at the end:

> *Which resounds,*
> *That you become manifest;*
> *And through all courses of time*
> *May there resound:*
> *Healing is through you.*

In these words about the healing power of Christ, we hear traces of the cosmic significance of the hierarchies' song, which resounds from the angels up to the Cherubim and Seraphim in the worship of the divine Son, the incarnate Logos. We hear that a healing power has come into our world as an offering from him; it comes to us through the mystery of the midnight birth on the night of all nights – the 'night of consecration'.[7]

Explanatory notes

The experience of Christmas night leads to a deepened sense of one's own cosmic origin. One begins to feel the truth of *ex Deo nascimur* become more concrete and individualised.

> On Christmas night we can, as we stand here upon earth, picture to ourselves how we are related through our physical, etheric and astral bodies to the threefold cosmos. Its etheric nature, shining so majestically, appears to us in the magic wonder of the night, in the blue of the heavens; its astral nature shines down out of the universe upon us, in the glittering stars. Then we can feel, in the holiness of this cosmic environment and in its relation to the earth, that our true ego-being has been placed into

these spatial conditions. And then we may gaze upon the Christmas Mystery – the new-born child, the representative of humanity on earth, who, inasmuch as he is entering into childhood, is born into this spatial world. In the fullness and majesty of this Christmas thought, as we gaze on the child that is born on Christmas Night, we can say: '*Ex Deo Nascimur* – I am born out of the divine, the divine that weaves and surges through the world of space.'[8]

The motif of the Christ-Sun comes up in various places in the rituals. In the Christmas Service for Children, for example, we hear of the 'sun-bright realm' of Christ. In this respect, in The Christian Community we hear echoes of the understanding prevalent during early Christianity. Many works of the early Church Fathers testify to a rejection of externalised worship of the sun, but at the same time show an integration of it at a higher level. Christ was recognised in the first centuries as the 'true sun', the 'Sun of Righteousness', and the new *sol invictus,* the invincible sun god. A text from the end of the third or beginning of the fourth century expresses this regarding Christmas day:

> But they also call (this day) the birthday of the unconquered Sun. Yet who is as unconquered as our Lord, who threw down death and conquered it? They may call this day the Birthday of Sol, but he alone is the Sun of righteousness, of whom the prophet Malachi said: There shall arise to you who fear his name the Sun of Righteousness, and there shall be healing under his wing.[9]

Early Christian sun worship often saw itself as a victory over the mysteries, but we can in fact see it as the *fulfilment* of the mysteries. Gregory of Nazianzus (*c.* 326–390), who called himself the 'choirmaster of the new mystery', held a Christmas sermon in Constantinople in AD 380 that began with the words: 'Again the darkness is past; again light rises.'

Another testimony to the connection between Christianity and ancient sun worship is from Maximus of Turin (*c.* 380 – *c.* 465):

> With the resurrection of our Saviour, there is a renewal not only of salvation for the whole human race, but of the brightness of the sun. If the sun grew dark at the passion of Christ, it must of necessity shine more brightly at his birth.[10]

In the development of the Church, the view prevailed that sun worship was a misplaced paganism in Christianity, but anthroposophy has provided the basis of knowledge to understand and appreciate the sun-mystery of Christ. The fact that anthroposophy and the ritual texts come from the same source is evident at this point: in the midnight epistle we hear of 'the Spirit's healing light of grace', while the children hear about 'Christ, the brightly shining Spirit Sun', which can be seen by the soul's eye from within.[11]

A modern inner Christmas experience can be found in a poem by Juan Ramon Jiménez (1881–1958), in which he speaks of 'the child of your I':

> Don't run, go slowly,
> It is only to yourself that you have to go!
> Go slowly, don't run,
> For the child of yourself, just born and eternal
> Cannot follow you.[12]

6. Epiphany

The Star of Grace

While the overall mood of the Christmas season is one of peace and silence, a special period, as if outside our usual sense of time, a season in which everything is illuminated by a higher reality, and God's love for humanity is renewed, the fundamental mood of the Epiphany season is quite different. From January 6 onwards, a new dynamic begins and time takes on a new character. The experience of Christ, born during Christmas, needs to be carried into the whole year. The fate of humanity depends on whether we succeed in this.

If we allow it, every experience can continue to resonate in us, not only in the sense of a chime that gradually fades into silence, but in the sense of an inspiration that can grow into a response to questions. What has the Christmas experience brought me this year? What seeds have been sown? What new impulses do I find within myself? The Epiphany weeks are the time to listen to the echo of all that the Christmas season evoked in us. We nurture with gratitude what was sown at Christmas, knowing that the new seeds that have sunk into our souls will one day bear fruit. Rudolf Steiner spoke of Christmas impulses needing 33 years to mature into Easter impulses.

The various meanings of Epiphany give it a special status and quality. In some parts of the world, it is one of the highest festivals, commemorating the baptism in the Jordan when the Son of God, the Christ, incarnated in the body of Jesus of Nazareth. What happened at Christmas with the infant Jesus – *et incarnatus est* – is only completed with the baptism that

6. EPIPHANY: THE STAR OF GRACE

Jesus receives through John the Baptist. Two other events are also traditionally commemorated on January 6: the adoration of the infant by the magi, and the wedding at Cana. These three events form a triad.

The commemoration of the visit of the priestly wise men in Bethlehem points to the *preparation* for Christ's incarnation. Gold, frankincense and myrrh symbolise and impart kingly wisdom, priestly piety and spiritual healing; thus these gifts prepared the path for Christ on earth.

The wedding at Cana, on the other hand, highlights the *results* of the baptism in the Jordan, insofar as it marks the beginning of Christ's work as the spirit of the sun among the people. As John reports: 'What Jesus did here in Cana of Galilee was the first of the signs through which he revealed his glory; and his disciples believed in him' (Jn 2:11). We can understand John to be saying that the divine glory of the sun shone on the disciples at that moment, opening their hearts to the reality of the Christ.

Just as the nature of time itself embraces with its two wings the past and the future in the eternal present, we can think of the Epiphany period as a triad of these three connected events: the magi's presentation of their offerings, the baptism in the Jordan and the wedding at Cana.

The epistle of the Epiphany season draws a wide arc from the macrocosmic appearance of the star of grace to the intimate microcosmic human life in Christ germinating in our depths.

> *Out of world-wide spaces*
> *Appeared the star of grace*
> *To join heart's-warming*
> *To spirit-enlightenment*
> *In the human being.*

At the beginning of the epistle, the way we lift our inner gaze to the heavens from which the star of grace appeared can remind us of how Zechariah, the father of John the Baptist, praised the light streaming from above to bless those in darkness below: 'the rising sun will come to us from heaven to shine on those living in darkness and in the shadow of death, to guide our feet into the path of peace' (Lk 1:78f). Grace itself takes shape above us, condensing out of the spiritual world, approaching and harmonising with our human world.

Now it is no longer a vision of the future as it was with Zechariah, for what he foresaw has already taken place: grace has become human in Jesus Christ. We can look up and remember that the star of grace *has truly* appeared, changing the world from the ground up.

At Christmas, what we can think of as a 'holy script' appeared above and on the altar, including the sequence of letters K M B (or C M B). As mentioned earlier, there are various complementary interpretations of what these signs mean.[1] Considering their connection to the three kings, why are the three letters no longer visible above the altar during Epiphany? They have disappeared externally in order to be brought to new life within us. The Christmas contemplation of the spiritual realities of these letters and the essential characteristics of the priest-kings become conscious and increasingly permeate us during this season. In this sense, Epiphany calls us to discover and embrace our own inner kingship.

> *Into the light of grace*
> *Into the Christ-star's*
> *Grace-bestowing ray*
> *Our souls*
> *Devoted to the eternal Father-will*
> *Would enter in humility.*

How are we to enter into the light of the star of grace? The Act of Consecration offers us the chance to practise this. We enter the chapel and approach the altar space, and in the course of the service, Christ's light of grace streams with increasing strength into the sacrament and flows towards us. In active surrender to the divine will, we can experience a higher freedom.

6. EPIPHANY: THE STAR OF GRACE

We are then asked to enter into the light of grace of the altar and open our souls, raising our inner gaze to the star of grace. We then hear the story of the incarnation of Christ again – but this time with an emphasis on the star. It is the *star* that calls the angels to communicate the good news to the wise priest-kings, that heavenly grace itself will become an epiphany; the star will become a human being.

> *May the holy Act of Consecration*
> *Be fulfilled*
> *In the upward glance of the soul*
> *To the star*
> *Which called the angels*
> *To announce*
> *To the wise of the world*
> *The grace-appearance*
> *Of the world's light.*

We gather in the chapel to pray together, for the sacrament is essentially a great prayer. At the same time, the sacrament is closely bound to the Christian festive year. It is a living being. At Christmas, the ritual is fulfilled and strengthened from the divine side. In the Epiphany season, the sacrament is newly embraced and practised from the human side. The grace of Christmas awakens and strengthens anew the strength of the sacrament in us. This divine force in human beings arises from the prayerful turning of the will towards God, from the warmed heart that beats for the star of grace and from the enlightened spiritual consciousness.

The epistle speaks in marvellously simple words about 'the heart's light of our prayer' longingly radiating towards the heavenly light in order to meet and unite with it.

> *May the heart's light of our prayer*
> *Meet yearningly*
> *The world-light of the star of grace.*

The sacrament is the meeting point of these two streams of light: the cosmic light of grace and the heart's light radiating from human beings. What we began to experience at Christmas lives on as the star of grace, which is the soul of Christ himself. Inspired by Christmas, we give birth to a response composed of light from our innermost being, 'the heart's light of our prayer'. This whole event leads to a kind of communion. The goal of the sacrament is revealed to us in the Epiphany epistle: that the 'life in Christ' may increasingly awaken, arise and grow stronger within us. The human soul, gifted with Christ, learns to see: the 'spirit-ray' of the star of grace becomes the eye of the soul. Epiphany becomes human, and we ourselves become the place of all future epiphany.

And life in Christ
Arise within us
When into the soul-eye penetrates
The spirit-ray of the star of grace.

Following the Creed there is an inserted prayer; like at Christmas and Easter, it is spoken by the priest facing the congregation, and articulates the basic structure of the Epiphany event: a proclamation from the divine world and the existential response of the human being. The special significance of the festival of Epiphany is voiced in this inserted prayer, which begins by summarising the divine message regarding humankind's salvation. This proclamation was made 'star-radiant'. These simple words hold such profound meaning: the activity of the Cherubim in the zodiac, the formation of special aspects or constellation of planets, and the wise men's recognition and understanding of the celestial language of the stars, night after night, devoted to the world above.

The worlds of spirit
Star-radiant
Announced
To seeking human souls
The right way of salvation

6. EPIPHANY: THE STAR OF GRACE

Where are the human souls today seeking to discern the work of divine spirits through the stars? Where are the people who sense the secrets of the starry world and seek to unravel them? It is possible and important for every human being to be a stargazer – or to become one again. The ones who cease searching are in danger of forgetting their origin in the starry world and of denying the eternal in themselves. Seeking, we reach out towards the heavens, and the heavenly world reveals to us through its messengers 'the right way of salvation'.

> *May human souls*
> *Radiating heart's love*
> *Find the guiding*
> *World-star of grace*
> *In the divine-warm*
> *Shining of salvation.*

It is worth noting that there is no mention of the way leading *to* salvation! No, the way itself – the way of Christ ('I am the way') – *is* the salvation. Buddha had already taught this truth of the way, thus preparing humanity for Christianity. And yet, how surprising this is after Christmas! By the end of the Christmas season, the world seems to stand still. Above it all rests the eternal splendour of the Christ's 'brightly shining spiritual sun', as we hear in the children's Christmas service. And now, in the Epiphany season, salvation is proclaimed as something that is only on the way, as if it is only in the walking itself that we attain the goal. The desire to 'have it all' is contrary to the spirit of true Christianity. The 'become!' of the Advent season returns at Epiphany in walking 'the right way of salvation'. It is a profound experience for each of us to feel we are on the right path, our own path, in contact with our higher being.[2]

The Epiphany inserted prayer that is spoken to the congregation culminates in an intercession of the divine world for humanity: that we may find the world's star of grace. The condition for this finding – which happens in the seeking itself – is that the heavenly star's seed in our hearts begin to open, and that our hearts themselves begin to stream out love. Then they become 'heart-sighted', and their rays illuminate what would otherwise remain obscured. Everything depends on our hearts beginning to illuminate what is still shadowed, particularly that they show us the star of Christ, which in turn lights up the way to the divine Father and his angels, the way to all creation and the way to ourselves.

This whole event is immersed in a vessel of warmth in which the Christmas light can find its creative echo and shine forth transformed. Epiphany builds bridges between heaven and earth, between light and warmth, between widths of the world and the intimacy of the heart. On these bridges appears the genius of humanity, looking up to the mighty revelation of the hierarchies – 'The worlds of Spirit ... announced' – and at the same time looking down in intercession to the human world: 'May human souls ... find the guiding world-star of grace.'

We can sense that we are not alone in the transition from the Christmas revelation to the trials of the new year. The Epiphany angel accompanies us in expectation and hope that the morning star rise in our hearts, and that Epiphany become our own future.

The history of the Epiphany epistle is noteworthy in this context. After work in the congregations started in autumn of 1922, the first Christmas for The Christian Community was imminent. In Advent 1922, Rudolf Steiner gave the priesthood the epistles for Christmas, but not yet for Epiphany.

In the course of 1923, Rudolf Steiner decided to organise a conference that represented a completely new beginning for anthroposophical work; Rudolf Steiner – until then not a member of the Anthroposophical Society – placed himself at the head of the newly founded society. All this took place in the light of the Christmas season. The Epiphany epistle was also born in this spiritually concentrated time, for immediately after the Christmas Conference ended in the first days of January 1924, Rudolf Steiner handed over the Epiphany texts to one of the priests at the

6. EPIPHANY: THE STAR OF GRACE

Christmas Conference. They were then hurriedly passed on to all the priests to be incorporated in the sacrament from January 6, 1924.

There are traces of an inner connection between that Christmas Conference and the Epiphany texts. In the closing words of the Christmas Conference, Rudolf Steiner urged the participants to carry their warm hearts, in which the spiritual foundation stone of the renewed Anthroposophical Society had been laid, out into the world for powerful, healing work. He showed that help would illuminate their heads, coming to them directly from the goals that the Christmas Conference participants want to serve. At the end of his address, he comes to the motif of the 'good star', with the plea that it might reign over all future activities that arise out of the spirit of the Christmas Conference:

> And help will be vouchsafed to you, enlightening your heads in what you would fain direct with single purpose. We will set about this with all possible strength. And if we prove to be worthy of this aim we shall see that a good star will hold sway over what is willed from here. Follow this good star, my dear friends! We shall see whither the gods will lead us by the light of this star.[3]

This is followed once again by part of the last verse of the Foundation Stone Meditation, like a quintessence of the Christmas Conference:

> O Light Divine
> O Sun of Christ!
> Warm thou our hearts,
> Enlighten thou our heads.

The triad of the divine light of the Christ-Sun, of the warming of hearts and the illumination of heads, is the crown and summary of the Foundation Stone Meditation of the Anthroposophical Society, which was founded anew during the 1923 Christmas

Conference. The same triad resounds throughout the Epiphany epistle of the Consecration of the Human Being. Thus, the Christmas mysteries continue on, enveloped in the harmony of 'the Christ-star's grace-bestowing ray', the warming of the heart and the illumination of the mind. If we listen to the last verse of the Foundation Stone Meditation and the Epiphany epistle together, we can sense their common source: the Christ's sunlit kingdom.

The Epiphany epistle brings the deepest spiritual experiences into the Christian sacraments. This epistle shows particularly clearly that The Christian Community as a movement for religious renewal represents the uniting of the esoteric and the exoteric. This is its objective task, for as Rudolf Steiner stated, 'The Christian Community is established on spiritual soil by spiritual beings in reality.'[4]

Explanatory notes

Every star is – spiritually speaking – a gateway for the working of spiritual beings. These workings are soul expressions from the spiritual world, and only by feeling into them as such is our gaze to the starry heavens a spiritual one. The love of the cosmos for humankind reveals itself in the starlight:

> Every star that we see glittering in the heavens is in reality a gate of entry for the astral. Wherever the stars shine towards us, the astral also shines. Look at the starry heavens in their manifold variety ... In all this wonderful configuration of radiant light, the invisible and supersensible astral body of the cosmos makes itself visible to us.
>
> For this reason, we must not view the world of stars unspiritually ...
>
> Think how living it all becomes when we know that the stars are an expression of the love with which the astral

cosmos works upon the etheric cosmos – for this is to express it with perfect truth.

The astral shines most intensely: it shines down to the earth through the stars, from the 'sun star'. The love of the starry world is like a cosmic caress:

> Now we see the stars as expressions of something real. I compared their action to a gentle stroking. It is the spirit selfhood behind them that lovingly strokes – only in this case it is not a single being but the whole world of the hierarchies ... In the same way, when I gaze up into the far reaches of the universe and look upon the stars, they are the living utterance of the hierarchies, kindling astral feeling. When I gaze into the blue depths of the firmament, I perceive in it the outward revelation of the etheric body which is the lowest member of the whole world of the hierarchies.[5]

7. Passiontide

Know Yourself

During Passiontide, the ritual texts confront us with deep questions about the meaning and nature of our humanity. At no other time of the year does it become so drastically clear to us that we as humans are imperfect beings. This is very difficult for modern human beings to accept; looking at our own imperfection can all too easily be felt as moral condemnation. The Passiontide epistle does not look at our personal weaknesses, but at the general, fundamental deficits of human beings. Out of self-knowledge and a deep affirmation of our own being, the inner call may be heard, 'Change your life!' It helps to keep in mind that only full acceptance of our imperfection can truly lead to change.

It may be useful here to remember the primal causality principle that became effective at the beginning of human development. At the beginning of the Old Testament, we hear that the human being is 'in principle' a divine idea that spiritual beings conceived and then formed – as opposed to a random product of evolution: 'Then God said, "Let us make mankind in our image, in our likeness".' (Gn 1:26).

The biblical myth continues to tell of the human being falling away from its divine origin in a process of continual entanglement in matter. The created human being forgets the divine origin – the 'likeness to God' disappears from his inner gaze. The reverse is also true: the divine world searches in vain for the paradisal human being: 'But the Lord God called to the man, "Where are you?"'(Gn 3:9).

7. PASSIONTIDE: KNOW YOURSELF

The Passion epistle is a rereading of the beginning of the Old Testament with a view to modern self-knowledge, a depth psychology that is held up to us like a mirror. It points us to the rediscovery of the worth of the human being, or as the sociologist Hans Joas put it, the 'sacredness of the person'. In the Passion epistle we can find a guide to our process of plumbing our own depths; we may feel it challenging us with the question of whether we are ready to practise the kind of self-knowledge, which, in the ritual context, becomes self-strengthening on the path to true humanity.

This act of looking at oneself in the mirror, however, presents two clear dangers: arrogance and despair – or in other words, overconfidence and depression. We need to look between these two tendencies to find as true an image of ourselves as possible. The realisation that we as human beings have come away from our original image and that our current self-image is missing something essential can be a fruitful starting point on our search for a new wholeness.

The Passion epistle voices a divine diagnosis of the human being, doing so in the spirit of truth and assistance, without moral reproach to the individual human being. Just as every illness that goes unrecognised eludes healing, so every diagnosis can be the starting point for healing. This epistle sheds light on the fundamental deficit that we all share – the 'sickness of sin' – as an infection of evil, which is connected to our bodily constitution being subject to disease and death. Seeing and articulating this painful diagnosis so clearly – without accusation, but with love – can, in fact, be the beginning of a healing.

The epistle's diagnosis begins by addressing us: 'O human soul'. We can interpret this appellation in two ways: on the one hand, it implies that we are not human in the full sense of the word. We are reminded of how many *inhumane* acts take place on a daily basis. On the other, hearing 'O human soul' can also feel like a recognition of the best in us, just as the Yiddish saying, *he was a real Mensch,* connotes awe and wonder for the person in question having truly fulfilled his potential. The 'O' opens up a solemn spiritual space to contemplate what it means to be a human being – a space that stretches from the original divine archetype of the human being to the future hope of a truly human humanity, to which every Act of Consecration of the Human Being contributes.

What follows may surprise us because we are not aware of it. We all have parts of our mind that we are not aware of but which are nevertheless active within us – that which we understand as our subconscious. There is another part of us that resides not 'below' our awareness (sub), but above it (supra), which we can call the 'supraconscious': this is the part of our soul that is connected to Christ.[1]

The epistle opens up both realms to us. Firstly, the area that has not yet been touched and redeemed by Christ: the empty heart! This image draws attention to all our actions that are not fed entirely from the heart. There are plenty of moments in our life when we exhibit – metaphorically speaking – a heart of stone. At the same time, it can make us aware that we have a certain power over our heart: we can decide when and where we direct it, what we 'attach' it to, how much we involve it in our actions.

The epistle tells us that the place of our heart is empty. Was it always empty? Even if we don't consciously remember it, we can imagine a time when it was full to the brim: both in our own early childhood, and in the childhood of humanity. Young children are still filled with an echo of their divine life before birth and can sometimes even articulate their awareness of what is 'above us'. When we are 'expelled' from the paradise of innocence, we lose this awareness, exchanging it for our ordinary, adult consciousness of the earthly world. In the language of the epistle, we lose 'the spirit that wakens' us, and live as if asleep. We can only fully regain this spirit at Pentecost.

O human soul,
Empty is the place of your heart,
You have lost
The spirit that wakens you

In the depths of our souls, however, we are not completely satisfied with the world of the senses being our only reality. A deep longing lives in us. As Ernst Bloch articulated in his *Principle of Hope,* our daydreams are the gateway to a hope for a brighter future. Longing for a renewed awakening of our inner being lives in our blood, which is the carrier of our I. Ultimately, we are not satisfied with merely settling in the earthly realm and thereby denying our spiritual home and divine origin. In our breath, which was experienced as spirit-filled in the ancient wisdom-filled cultures of Asia, we no longer feel anything of Brahman, the primal spirit. All that is no more. It is up to us to wake up and realise the intimate connection with the divine that has been lost to us. It was an interweaving that was as strong in our awareness as our breath is, with a similar effect of bringing new life into our blood with every breath. The epistle provides a window into this loss. What seems 'normal' is not healthy. We have fallen to earth and begin to sense what we are missing. Opening up to this reality, we can be gripped by a deep, supra-personal sadness about the state of humanity – namely about our distance from God. The Passiontide epistle reminds us to take this seriously, not to pass over it too quickly or deceive ourselves about it.[2]

> *Longing for the spirit's*
> >   *Awakening*
> *Wells within your blood*
> *Want through*
> >   *Loss of the spirit*
> *Surges within your breath –*
> *Mournful awaiting*
> *Is the part*
> *Of your consciousness.*

The multilayered character of spiritual reality is reflected in the way the passages from the gospels read during Passiontide give us strength and courage to endure what the epistle so harshly confronts us with. We hear the story of the feeding of the five thousand (Jn 6), a number that refers to our time – the fifth post-Atlantean cultural epoch. In our state of deprivation, we experience the depth of the miraculous nourishment that 'the Lord of life', as the 'bread of the world', pours into our emptiness.

Another gospel reading during these weeks is the story of the adulteress (Jn 8). By confronting the accusers instead of the woman, Christ reveals that we are all affected by the consequences of the original sin: 'Let him who is without blame among you cast the first stone at her!' Those with life experience walk away affected – inwardly, their awakened conscience tells them: 'We have no right to hold ourselves above this woman.' Standing alone in the centre with the woman who had feared for her life, Christ gives her a new orientation by which she might lead her life in the future.

The accounts of the miraculous feeding and the salvation of the adulteress bring the light of hope into our darkness, helping us to bear the serious diagnosis of our godforsaken and guilt-laden humanity.

In the fourth week of Passiontide, Holy Week, the divine diagnosis intensifies into an existential drama. The empty heart now begins to burn, but this burning remains cold. Our whole existence is now characterised by spiritual cold: we live in the 'Spirit-forsaken House of Earth'. 'You have a reputation of being alive, but you are dead' (Rv 3:1). Sometimes, at the onset of a storm, it can become dark in the middle of the day so suddenly that we almost doubt the existence of the sun and the blue sky. During Holy Week our inner state is – objectively seen – as gloomy as that moment is outside. It is not necessarily perceptible in our mood, for this goes beyond personal melancholy: in our very blood, we are distant from God, despite the spring, despite the blossoms, despite the birdsong. 'Sorrow trickles in your blood.' Can we let that feeling in and endure it? Can we recognise what our blind spot hides from us? Can we look at ourselves once a year from that divine perspective and allow ourselves to be told how things really are for us spiritually? Can we hear the truth about ourselves spoken by the One who looks at us realistically, but at the same time with infinite love – who wants to feed us precisely because we are spiritually starving, who wants to lift us up and strengthen us because we have fallen?

> *O human soul,*
> *Burning is the place of your heart*
> *You live in the cold*
> *Spirit-forsaken*
> *   House of earth –*
> *Sorrow trickles*
> *In your blood*

The seed of healing lies in accepting this diagnosis. We close ourselves off to healing when we refuse the bitter vinegar of self-knowledge.

The epistles of Passiontide and Holy Week are radical, in that they get at the root of our existence – but they also lead to hope. We look ahead to the tomb, which gives us hope, because new light, new nourishment and new strength will arise from it even if we still have to go through grief:

> *Hope alone*
> *Streams in your breath –*
> *From a grave of hope*
> *   A ray of grief*
> *Penetrates your*
> *   Gaze.*

This combination of words and sentences cannot be comprehended logically, and yet the contrasting way many elements resound together feels familiar: hope and grave, mourning and light, our view out into the world, and that which meets our gaze, permeating us. Hope is born out of mourning.

The Epistle and Gospel Reading are followed by the calm and balance of the Creed, which draws a grand arc from the foundation of the world through Christ's death and resurrection to the ultimate hopes of humankind. Our response to the diagnosis of the Passiontide epistle, which has shaken us to the core, can grow out of this calm. The inserted Passion prayer after the Creed is full of an honesty born of being shaken and disenchanted. It is a cry for mercy and help, a plea for understanding. Perhaps we can hear in it an echo of the disciples' outcry that resounds in our souls at this point: 'Who then can be saved?' (Lk 18:26).

> *Look, O Spirit*
> *Of the worlds afar*
> *And of the earth near,*
> *Not on the sting of evil*
> *In the earthly human heart*
> *Look on the tempting power*
> *Of our weakness –*

If the Godhead only looked at our human weaknesses and failings, it would soon despair of us. Let us remember what the Bible says very early on: 'The Lord regretted that he had made human beings on the earth, and his heart was deeply troubled.' (Gn 6:6). But we may ask God to 'Look on the tempting power of our weakness'. Superhuman powers of evil are involved – then and now – who are far superior to humans in their spiritual rank. St Paul speaks of 'the powers of this dark world and ... the spiritual forces of evil in the heavenly realms' (Eph 6:12). They have taken advantage of our weaknesses, implanted in us the 'sting of death' (1Cor 15:56), and pitted us against God at a time when we were not yet in a position to see through and resist the temptations. Plato had an awareness of this sting, from which we must guard ourselves with all our strength.[3]

Since then, evil forces have been at work in humanity. We innocently became guilty; yet we still have to bear the consequences and seek to transform them through the power of Christ.

To do this, it is necessary that we pass through the nadir of self-knowledge and openly recognise the basic situation of our fallen human nature rather than avoid this bitter recognition. 'My self lies lamenting on the ground.'

Only from this place of powerlessness can a resurrection take place. Is this innermost dimension of the spiritual Passion accessible to us? Can we feel our way into the horror of having rejected and killed the Saviour? Did we not join in the cry: 'Crucify him, crucify him'? And how many offences are being committed today against every creature, to which we close our eyes, but which he feels and suffers! Despair can fill us when we realise that we continue to crucify him every day, even unintentionally. This is the lowest point – we feel ourselves 'lamenting on the ground' – from which the only direction to go is up. Yet it is precisely in this moment of bare truth that healing begins to take place: the deep churning of the soul is a cleansing process that creates a nothingness out of which something new can emerge. We can sense his presence in this nothingness. The silent lament can stir up and purify the soul, then ultimately clarify and calm it.

My self lies
Lamenting on the ground
Raise it, O Spirit
Of the worlds afar
And of the earth near.

Just as we would call for help when we have fallen and cannot get back up on our own, we call upon the divine for help to inwardly raise us. And how awe-inspiring is the experience of being uplifted with Christ's help and finally being able to stand upright again. The Passiontide epistle leads us through an unsparing diagnosis into radical self-knowledge, to culminate in the plaintive plea for the elevation of our I. This process is accompanied by the love of Christ. The inner Easter experience is being prepared.

Explanatory notes

According to Genesis, we are created in the image of God. Early Christian theologians saw two different aspects in this: on the one hand, Augustine (354–430) and others interpreted this as a merciful resemblance to God, while on the other hand, Gregory of Nyssa (*c.* 335 – *c.* 395), for example, based his understanding of the *imago Dei* on the co-creative freedom of the human being. Gregory looks to the future in this, seeing the human beings' ultimate potential. Our long and arduous path to freedom is to be fulfilled in a new relationship with God. In a frequently quoted passage from his *Life of Moses,* Gregory wrote, 'Spiritual birth is the result of a free choice, which implies that we are, in a certain sense, our own parents. We create ourselves as we want to be; we model ourselves through our will according to the model we choose.' According to Gregory, we owe our possibility of freedom to our likeness to God.

The Gospel of John speaks of a further, higher level of freedom. 'If the Son sets you free, you will be free indeed' (8:36). Christ is the 'image of the invisible God' (Col 1:15), or as we hear during the Transformation in the Act of Consecration, the 'Son who has his being in love'. As such, he unites in himself the paradox of the future: perfect freedom and perfect love.

In becoming a Christian, we can restore our likeness to God and develop it further. *Ad imaginem Dei* – 'in the image of God' – is the human being's natural disposition. The world rests on the courage of the gods to take the human risk fully consciously: 'O human soul ... you have lost the Spirit that wakens you.'

We find the motif of the thorn in St Paul. During his imprisonment, he wrote of the voice speaking to him at his Damascus experience: 'Saul, Saul, why do you persecute me? It is hard for you to kick against the goads [literally *stings*]'. (Ac 26:14). In the Second Letter to the Corinthians (12:7), Paul speaks of a sting or thorn in his body that protects him from arrogance: 'In order to keep me from becoming conceited, I was given a thorn in my flesh, a messenger of Satan, to torment me'.

There has been a lot of speculation about this passage. What was the illness that afflicted Paul? According to Rudolf Steiner, Paul was a 'premature soul', as if born before his time, and as such, experienced materialism like a thorn:

> Civilised humanity has a thorn in its side. St Paul speaks of this thorn a good deal, and what he says is prophetic. He was a particularly advanced individual – most people didn't begin to feel the thorn until the seventh century. This thorn will lodge itself deeper and deeper in us, will influence us more and more. People who are strongly affected by this thorn nowadays – who suffer from this ailment, for that is what it is – become atheists, deny the divine. Every single person belonging to modern, western civilisation has a predisposition to atheism; whether he gives himself up to it is another matter. ...
>
> This sickness has brought about a stronger force of attraction between the human soul and body than was previously the case, and than our innate human nature would otherwise give rise to. The soul has as it were been welded onto the body.[4]

8. Easter

In the Realm of the Heart

The realm of Easter is an open secret. The encounter of the two disciples with the risen Christ on the road to Emmaus represents the classic situation. The earthly events that have just taken place have not yet become transparent to them. They are preoccupied with Jesus' crucifixion, death and burial, while the risen Christ is still hidden from them. With the resurrection, Christ Jesus became the resplendent centre of a new kingdom, as, for instance, Grünewald depicted in his famous Isenheim painting, *The Resurrection of Christ*.

The Gospel portrays the two disciples walking, carrying the events of Golgotha in their souls like an open wound (Lk 24:13–32). Their greatest hopes have been shattered, and they have fled from Jerusalem, seeking distance. A stranger comes upon them, apparently unaware of everything that has happened, so they try to describe the iniquitous events to him. Two different realities collide. Christ has to realise that, despite the woman at the empty tomb being able to perceive him as her beloved teacher, his current Easter reality is still hidden to the disciples. 'How foolish you are, and how slow to believe all that the prophets have spoken.'

Their continuing on the path to Emmaus is at the same time an inner path of knowledge culminating in the words, 'Did not the Messiah have to suffer these things and then enter his glory?' This entering his glory, this revelation was the key to the disciples' understanding. Then, when he broke the bread with them, the disciples took the step in perception from death to resurrection, 'Were not our hearts burning within us?

8. EASTER: IN THE REALM OF THE HEART

Even today, we all still have to keep searching anew for the entry point to Easter. We enter the chapel on Easter morning with a disposition of seeking, perhaps a quiet premonition. May we be open-minded and awake of heart, because that is where Easter is. We notice this upon seeing the altar space – so different from the feeling of inward star-gazing of Christmas and Epiphany, or the dark stillness of Passiontide – as if the red has suddenly burst out of the black to call out to us inaudibly: 'Wake up, sleeper, rise from the dead, and Christ will shine on you' (Eph 5:14).

The crucial question now is whether we are ready to hear, not in the outward sense, but in the inner sense. 'I hear your message, but faith fails me', says Faust as a representative of the modern individual.[1] Faith here basically means openness of heart, a willingness to really engage with the 'unheard of'. The first words of the Easter epistle sound formidable – certainly as monumental as the content they reveal to us:

The grave is empty
The heart is full

These few words really say it all. Firstly, it is the same message that the women heard at the empty grave, and now we, too, stand before the empty tomb that the altar symbolises. And then comes the moment when Easter bridges are built – from then to now, from outside to inside, from the specific place of Jerusalem to every open heart: 'The heart is full.' Between the two statements, a question can arise: where is he, who no longer is in the grave? This question is answered by what follows: the heart is full *of him*. Can we realise this? Can it become a real experience, from an assertion to an act of the heart?

In the Eastern Orthodox Church there is the wonderful tradition of lighting the Easter candle to receive the message, 'Christ is risen' (*the grave is empty*). Upon hearing the message, the individual responds affirmatively: 'He is truly risen' (*the heart is full*). Everyone says it in their own way, otherwise it remains a general formula without becoming an individual, existentially experienced truth.

The Easter thought that pervades the words of the epistle so vividly can deeply warm our inner being. The basic fact of the fulfilled heart is deepened in a 'sacramental physiology' and made conscious to us: a new warmth has entered the human heart and dissolved all that was hardened within it. We are amazed to be told that our heartbeat quietly changes and our heart begins to beat for the Risen One. This in turn has an effect on our soul, in which a rejoicing, healing power spreads.

Warmth changes
The beat of the heart
Into jubilating
Healing power

The heart is transformed from a perceiving organ into a strength-giving organ, becoming a source for 'heart work', which can be understood as activity that pulsates with the essence of Easter. The blood that courses through our heart is the carrier of our higher spiritual being. This enables us to be connected to the life and movement of the cosmos, which also has a soul and spirit.[2] The spirit of the cosmos, the Logos, through whom everything has come into being, embraces us from within at Easter, graciously renewing us down to our blood and breath. Christ's Easter activity in the unconscious depths of our being allows us to feel a new reality in his words, 'I am the resurrection and the life' (Jn 11:25).

The weaving of your blood
Is fulfilment
The surging of your breath
Is comfort of spirit

From the great cosmic Easter events, the epistle now speaks to us of our ordinary life on earth – our breath, our blood, our warmth. After the desolation and darkness of Passiontide, we can use the comforting and encouraging words it offers us in this area

8. EASTER: IN THE REALM OF THE HEART

of our everyday life. Because the living realm of Easter often slips from our consciousness, the epistle reminds us:

The comforter of your earth-existence
Walks in the spirit
Before you.[3]

After the 'Christ in you', the epistle resumes, but the priest moves to the centre facing the altar. It is as if the whole congregation is speaking: the words come from the mouth of the priest, but it is the *heart* that speaks, encompassing the hearts of all those present. (Something similar was mentioned with respect to the Christmas midnight service, when the spiritual light shines upon us after our inmost heart has engaged in anticipating prayer.) The human heart harbours a mystery. On the one hand, it holds our very own innermost being, and what comes 'from the heart' comes from our innermost being. On the other, it is also something that does not belong to us, for the heart is also an enclave of the divine world within us, a place where the spiritual world makes a temporary home within us.

My heart praises
The Spirit of God
My spirit feels
The Vanquisher of Death

Now, at Easter, we can experience Christ uniting the often separated soul qualities of mind-clarity and feeling-warmth. The spirit senses the act of Christ, his overcoming of death as it is expressed in the Creed, 'Then he overcame death after three days.' This is the full dimension of the resurrection: not only that he rose again, but that he *overcame death* once and for all, and for all people. With each new celebration of this festival, we are allowed to enter more and more into the realm of Easter and affirm the following lines with our whole being:

> *Joy is the streaming power*
> *Of my breath*
> *Grace is the living might*
> *Of my blood.*

Only a few times during the festival year does the priest turn and address the congregation with a special prayer. The act of turning and facing the congregants is otherwise reserved for the 'Christ in you'. One can thus say that what is spoken to the congregation is now spoken out of the spirit of this Christ greeting. This part of the Easter epistle spoken directly to the congregation accompanied by a special gesture of blessing, known from ancient Egyptian culture as the Ka gesture.[4] It radiates calm and blessing power, which emphasises the importance of the words. The message simultaneously gives us a task and gives meaning to our lives on earth:

> *Your word go forth*
> *Spirit-wakened*
> *From your mouth.*
> *Christ is risen to you*
> *As the meaning of the earth.*

These words present us with an Easter mission, for they express a supplication that we should take to heart, to save the living Word.[5] It can bring to mind the proclamation of the Risen One to the disciples, which we hear at the end of the Easter Gospel: 'Go into all the world and preach the gospel to all creation' (Mk 16:15). This commission is now being carried out. As participators in the Act of Consecration, we are all called on to resurrect the Word within us.

Let us remember Christ's statement: 'Heaven and earth will pass away, but my words will never pass away' (Lk 21:33). The foundation for these Easter words is his resurrection. A new world is being prepared in the Word: a world that will not perish at the end of our time on earth, but will be born anew out of what is dying.

8. EASTER: IN THE REALM OF THE HEART

The resurrection of Jesus Christ is also the foundation for our life on earth to be meaningful. We hear the words 'to you' added to the angels' succinct Easter message at the empty tomb, 'He is risen': Christ is risen to us, to the people. We can hear in this his great love for us: he sacrificed himself, conquered death and established eternal life in the resurrection. In this way, humanity and the earth have received their great meaning, for Christ has become 'the meaning of the earth'.[6]

The inserted prayer that follows the Creed can be heard as the epistle's extension and continuation. A deeply joyful confession of the cosmic Christ resounds, singing the cosmic dimension of the Easter event. The priest raises his arms to the image of the exalted Christ. All that follows is spoken from the perception of the living Christ who is present in the ambit of the earth. Living with these words forms the eyes of the soul and the ears of the spirit, which allow us to perceive the presence of the living Christ more and more.

> *Jubilating*
> *In delight*
> *Is the air around the earth*
> *Living*
> *In the spirit-radiant*
> *Power of the sun*
> *Is the breath of the earth*
> *Christ has entered*
> *Our rejoicing*
> *Pulse of life.*

The 'breath of the earth' is permeated with new, inner 'power of the sun', so that, as Christian Morgenstern wrote, 'it, too, may one day become a sun'.[7] Divine love, in the form of Christ, reigns above all the doom and destruction that is taking place and will continue to take place on earth. Not for a moment could our life exist on earth without his divine solar life-force. These resurrection powers put our devoted souls into a state of bliss, which, spiritually speaking, is the inner state in which 'the heart beats only for the future'.[8] The human soul becomes an echo of the earth's surroundings. In devotion to the Easter mystery, the human soul finds spiritual seeds in body, soul and spirit that grow towards the future. In the body, it finds the seed of future resurrection – 'what has risen in power from chains of death.' In the soul, the seed lies in our will and sprouts out of the light and life of the Christ, strengthening us for our earthly tasks. The seed found in the I, in the spirit, is the healing power of Christ that dwells in us as potential.

> *We find*
> *In the delight*
> *Of our devoted souls:*
> *What is risen in power*
> *From chains of death*
> *What in the light is newborn*
> *In the life of Christ*
> *What heals the self*
> *In the ground of the soul.*

In their contradictory nature, the hymn-like words that then follow create awareness of the radical turnaround from Passiontide's death experience to the Easter resurrection experience.

> *Living is the soul*
> *Which was dead*
> *Shining is the self*
> *Which was dark*
> *Abounding is the spirit*
> *Which was closed.*

We know from the ancient mysteries that the resurrection mystery was shown to the neophyte in images after long, hard

8. EASTER: IN THE REALM OF THE HEART

preparation. These pictures were of the future: death and burial, passage through death, descent into the depths, ascent to the heights.[9] What was presented in ritualistic dramas in the mysteries took place on Golgotha as a real, external deed. The deed on Golgotha is God's sacrament in the human realm. This sacrament is the beginning of a continuous stream of deeds, for the Easter event weaves into every open human heart.

> *The grave of the soul*
> *Opens.*
> *The grave of the soul*
> *Becomes an altar.*

The last part of the inserted prayer speaks of the human soul as an altar, that is, as a meeting place of the heavenly with the human, a place for the working of the Risen One. This is where he can work for the salvation of humanity. The purpose of every external altar event is to build the altar of the soul, so that Christ can always fulfil the mystery of death and resurrection within us. It is a signature of Christianity in our time that this happens 'in human spirit light', in awake, devotional thinking, feeling and will towards others.

> *Christ offers*
> *At the soul-altar*
> *In human spirit light*
> *To the worlds afar*
> *To the earth near*
> *Now and beyond all cycles of time.*

Explanatory notes

Easter 1924 was the last Easter that Rudolf Steiner experienced on earth. On April 7, he began his famous watercolour painting *Easter,* which he finished on Holy Saturday, April 19. This picture, painted in powerful colours, expresses the theme that particularly preoccupied Rudolf Steiner in 1924 in connection with Easter: the cosmic aspect of Easter, which is also the mystery aspect.

A stream of spiritual life flowed out of the Christmas Conference into the renewal and deepening of Easter. The lecture series *The Easter Festival in Relation to the Mysteries* is a testimony to this. These four lectures took place from Holy Saturday to Easter Tuesday in 1924. In the last lecture Rudolf Steiner spoke of the task of reshaping Easter as an experience of humanity, linking the Easter lectures in this way to the Christmas Conference:

> I can therefore say, as on other occasions: Anthroposophy is a Christmas event, and in all its effects it is also an Easter event, a resurrection experience that is connected with a burial.[10]

In these Easter lectures it becomes apparent that in the foregoing year Rudolf Steiner had not only been working on creating a new Michael festival, but had also been developing a new understanding of the Michaelic character of the entire festival cycle. The annual cycle of festivals unites the cosmic aspects, the mystery aspects and freedom aspects on a new level: Easter is a new birth out of the spiritual forces of the sun. Carrying spiritual sun-forces into humanity, Christ releases human beings from the iron necessity of remaining subject to moon-forces through their physical birth.

> It is the force of Christ looking down on me through that cosmic, solar eye that enables me to make something of

myself during my life on earth through my inner freedom, something I could not have been, through the lunar forces which placed me here.

This consciousness that we could transform ourselves, could make something out of ourselves, is what people saw in the forces of the sun.[11]

We become evolving beings through the birth out of the sun. We reconnect with the cosmic power of the sun, which was reopened to us through Christ's resurrection. The inserted prayer says:

In the spirit-radiant
Power of the sun
Is the breath of the earth

By lifting ourselves up to this Easter sphere in an experiential way, we can feel a rebirth take place within ourselves. We may find,

What in the light is newborn
In the life of Christ.

In the last lecture of this series, Steiner talked about the burning of the Goetheanum in connection with the burning in 356 BC of the temple in Ephesus, one of the seven wonders of the world. As a result of the fire at that time, Steiner described 'a continuous Easter' as being inscribed in the 'etheric world dome' at Ephesus, where it became legible and accessible for the higher cognition. Like the physical temple in Ephesus, which became mere ruins as a result of the fire, the Goetheanum also fell victim to the flames and became a grave. If we look for the reality of the Goetheanum there, we will receive the same answer as the mystery priests in Ephesus once did:

'That which ye seek is no longer here, it is in your hearts, if only ye will open them to receive it in right way.'

Anthroposophy already dwells in human hearts, Humans have only to open their hearts to it in the right way.[12]

In the epistle it says:

The grave is empty
The heart is full

Our need for redemption can by no means be restricted to the moral level, for it relates to our fundamental constitution as a human being. We have lost the dimension of time and have become a mere spatial being:

> And from that world [beyond space] Christ came to humanity. At the time when Christianity was founded by Christ on earth, man had already been far too long confined to the mere *Ex Deo Nascimur,* he had become altogether bound up in it and had lost the realm of time. He had become a being who dwelt only in space. The reason why it is so hard for us to understand the traditions of older epochs, when we go back to them with the consciousness of present-day civilisation, is that they were restricted to the world of space and considered time only in spatial terms.
>
> But then Christ came and once more brought the element of time to humanity; and when the human heart, the human soul, the human spirit, unite themselves with Christ, then we can again receive the stream of time that flows through all eternity ... Christ gave time back again to human beings.

The human being can gain a share in this by learning to die in Christ, in order to have the opportunity to pass through death into a new life:

8. EASTER: IN THE REALM OF THE HEART

In addition to the *Ex Deo Nascimur,* we must find the *In Christo Morimur.* To the Christmas thought of *Ex Deo Nascimur* must be added the Easter thought of *In Christo Morimur.*[13]

By being able to receive Christ within ourselves, we can inwardly transform death, overcoming death in death itself.

9. Ascension

Traces of Heaven and Traces of Earth

The Ascension of Christ is the festival following the long Easter period. Probably no other festival is more distant to our modern consciousness than the celebration of an ascension to the heavens. The epistle for this period dispenses with the word 'Ascension', focusing instead on providing a window to the inner experience that this festival offers. It leads the soul in a comprehensive movement from the ground of being to an upward gaze at Christ, while at the same time crystallising the Ascension experience in the present. This event takes place in the here and now, albeit in the hidden realm of our sense world.

The epistle starts by evoking the image of the Father-Ground of all Being, then moves to the image of the mission of Christ and his victory over death on Golgotha.

> *Divine Father-Ground*
> *You who wield among all beings:*
> *You have sent him,*
> *And he has confirmed his sending*
> *Through teaching, suffering*
> *Through death and victory over death.*

Tracing this path in our consciousness makes us aware of his presence today in the inner realm of the outer world. He is there, but his being is at the same time beyond the threshold;

9. ASCENSION: TRACES OF HEAVEN AND TRACES OF EARTH

it is expanded, having shed the narrow confines of the human body, and has become comprehensive, like the being of the Father.

In the lines that follow, we hear that movement is an essential characteristic of the Ascension event.

> *He lives in earthly being,*
> *Transfiguring earthly being*
> *With heavenly being;*
> *We behold with*
> *Heart's power of vision*
> *His elevation to heavenly being*
> *For the sake of earthly being.*
> *May he dwell with us*
> *In that he dwells with you.*

It is the resurrection life forces of Christ, wrested from death, that flow into the dying earthly existence and interweave heaven with earth. Ascension is in truth a cosmic marriage of the earthly with the heavenly, insofar as what has been separated from the spirit shines anew with these life forces. This all happens for the salvation of earth existence.

The great life of the Risen One is able to encompass all these contrasts, so that dwelling with the Father becomes dwelling with us. This proximity to Christ that we experience leads to an increase in our spiritual strength, but strength is difficult to grasp with consciousness, because it belongs to the realm of our dormant will.

The Ascension epistle speaks of a new Christ-power in our souls, which emerges from his cosmic omnipresence, through which he 'bears and orders the life of the world', as we hear it said in the Consecration of the Human Being. We now want to take up this power in order to carry out the sacrament together, for the 'Christ in us' is the true celebrant of the Act of Consecration.

> *With his power in our souls*
> *We would fulfill*
> *The Act of Consecration*
> *Looking up to him.*

In ascending to the heights, Christ carries something new up with him. He himself embodies the fruits of his earthly mission, incorporating them into the divine world through his being. After the Creed, we hear the words of the inserted prayer.

> *Christ's power of soul*
> *Reveals itself*
> *In the heights,*
> *Into which he embodies*
> *Earthly being.*

When we incorporate or embody something, what we assimilate serves to preserve our bodily existence and contributes to the continuation of our life. When earthly existence is incorporated into the heights, it is similar to the intake of food: the divine world and its spiritual beings experience a kind of nourishment through what Christ has gained by living on earth. What has happened on earth takes on cosmic significance and can serve heavenly existence.

This raises a great question: What in earth existence is worthy of ascension? What can Christ carry up into his kingdom from us that would serve as a blessing for the development of the earthly world and the cosmos?

The Easter event creates ever-widening ripples that also encompass the depths. The essence of the Ascension event is that the existence of the Risen One has expanded to become part of the initial formation of a new heaven and a new earth. If the transfiguration on the mountain is the seed of the resurrection, the Ascension is its fruit.

The inner place of the Ascension event is the kingdom of the etheric Christ, which we could think of as his spiritual Galilee. At

9. ASCENSION: TRACES OF HEAVEN AND TRACES OF EARTH

the time of the actual Ascension, the disciples could not yet follow him there. He 'surpassed' their inner capacity, disappearing from their sight. They could not maintain the supernatural consciousness needed to accompany their Lord. Today, however, we are beginning to participate in his spiritual Galilee through the Christ in us:

> *The eyes of our souls*
> *Behold him*
> *In the being of the clouds*
> *Bestowing blessing*
> *On earthly being.*

This upward gaze to the cosmic Christ and the holy feeling of his nearness allow us to experience his presence ever more clearly, leading ultimately to a tender intuition.

The historical Last Supper becomes here a cosmic, eternal nourishment that enacts the lasting marriage of heaven and earth.[1] If we actively devote ourselves to the sacrament with Christ's strength in our souls, new organs of perception are gradually formed in us, which can lead to similar visions.

Our initial perceptions can allow the deeper soul forces, stunted by intellectual habits developed during the Age of Reason, to stir again. Praise, exaltation, gratitude and song can now come to the fore, and we sense that the intellect is no longer the soloist, dominating and silencing all the other soul forces. Now, warmed through with Christ forces, the intellect *enables* the soul – in clear knowing and out of a full heart – to praise, glorify and celebrate what it has recognised.

A new confession at the level of the consciousness soul germinates in this recognition. Knowing clarity, warm sympathy and devotional power are simultaneously united and developed within the integral consciousness, which thus leads to the modern discipleship of Christ:

> *Therefore our hearts*
> *Sound forth his praise*
> *And may our song of praise*
> *Follow his course,*
> *That we be*
> *Those who confess him*
> *Through all cycles of time.*

The word 'creed' comes from the Latin *credo,* 'I believe'. Creed has come to mean a statement of belief, a 'confession', yet its etymological root holds a deep secret: the word heart (*cor*) is hidden in the word *credo,* so that *credo* literally means 'I unite my heart with'. To believe something is to unite our heart with it. When we say 'I confess Christ', we are in fact saying, 'I unite my heart with Christ I give him a dwelling place in my heart,' so that he 'may dwell with us' by dwelling with the Father, as we heard in the epistle.

Ascension heralds the new coming of Christ: he 'will come back in the same way you have seen him go into heaven' (Ac 1:11).

Passiontide's self-surrender, Easter's deed on Golgotha and Ascension's movement progressively lead up to the impact of Pentecost.

9. ASCENSION: TRACES OF HEAVEN AND TRACES OF EARTH

Explanatory notes

The Mystery of Golgotha occurred as a spiritually objective act for all people, regardless of their belief or confession. This is the meaning of what we call the Ascension. But how is it for Christ himself – has he also experienced something new in himself?

> And the answer is, he did ... what he experienced – his ascent into a world still more exalted than the one in which he had previously had his being – this he revealed in his Ascension to those who were his companions on the earth.[2]

10. Pentecost

Flame of Spirit

The power of human initiative is called upon in the course of the festivals, and at Pentecost this begins on an individual level. The stream of blessings that we receive from Advent through Ascension can now become the source from which we, with our spiritual powers, can grow into and unite with the flaming activity of the Holy Spirit. The nature of the Spirit is such that it cannot be held or taken possession of. The 'original' Pentecost has withdrawn into the future, in order to be renewed from there again and again. We are called to echo the words of Friedrich Hölderlin when he wrote to his beloved Diotima, 'Daily I must call upon the vanished godhead.'[1]

The love of the Spirit awakens in us at Pentecost. Christ sends us the Spirit out of his union with God the Father: 'Now I am going to him who sent me ... Unless I go away, the Advocate will not come to you' (Jn 16:5, 7). This arrival of the Spirit – the Advocate or Helper – begins in our healed consciousness, which emerges, liberated, from its constriction in the sensory world and expanded by the inner Ascension. Out of his union with the Father, Christ sends the Spirit into our souls:

> *Christ sends*
> *Into our souls*
> *The Father-Ground's Spirit,*
> *Who heals*
> *As world-physician*
> *The weakness of souls*
> *And the infirmities of mankind.*

10. PENTECOST: FLAME OF SPIRIT

The Holy Spirit becomes the world physician, developing diagnosis and therapy for 'the infirmities of humankind'. May his strength overcome our weakness; may it penetrate our soul and heal our physical existence.

This healing process cannot happen without our openness to and understanding of the Spirit. Christ's love for us, out of which he has done everything until now, is what enables the Pentecostal spirit to blossom forth in us. Like the disciples, we, too, become able to understand the mission of Christ and, with deepest gratitude, we can marvel at its significance for the whole world.

At Pentecost it becomes particularly clear that the Act of Consecration is the future taking place in the present. What the individual – even the priest – is not yet able to do, happens in and through the sacrament. The Consecration of the Human Being can thus become a way for Pentecost to work in the present.

> *May the Spirit who brings healing*
> *Wield in the word of offering*
> *Blessing the deed of offering,*
> *That works*
> *In the Act of Consecration,*
> *That stems*
> *From Christ's ordaining*

The Pentecost epistle casts a special light on the fulfilment of the Act of Consecration. To the extent that we remain servants of the Word and devoted to the truth, our word can become a word of offering. The *word* of offering flows over into the *deed* of offering and elevates the sacrament to a place where the sacrificial deed of Christ on Golgotha comes alive. The blessing of the Holy Spirit fills the congregation when the words are heard that the Act of Consecration 'stems from Christ's ordaining'. Christ himself created this Spirit-vessel in order to fulfil anew what he promised, 'I am with you always, to the very end of the age' (Mt 28:20). The light-filled fulfilment of the sacrament that heals us profoundly is the Risen One lighting up in the now. This is Pentecost.

In the Gospel reading during Pentecost, we hear: 'Anyone who loves me will guard my Word ... Anyone who does not love me will not guard my Word' (Jn 14:24f, literal translation). This reveals the essence of Pentecost: this festival is characterised by the spirit of *mutual* love. The second part of the Pentecost epistle, the inserted prayer spoken between the Creed and the Offertory, can ignite this love in us directly:

> *Behold the flames*
> *They are the Spirit's revelation.*
> *So flame the word*
> *Of the Act of Consecration*
> *So flame the deed*
> *Of the Act of Consecration.*

What descended as divine fire on the disciples gathered devoutly at the original Pentecost can still – in those whose hearts are filled with Christ – 'kindle their being in the word of praise'. These few words say so much. Our divine essence does not ordinarily burn within us. Our essence – our actual, higher being – usually lies above us, out of reach. Pentecost, however, is the festival season that kindles that essence within us. The heart is full of these flames, and our mouth can likewise overflow with them.

> *The flames stream heavenward;*
> *They stream forth from human hearts,*
> *Which filled with Christ*
> *Kindle their being*
> *In the word of praise*
> *Filled with the Spirit*
> *He has summoned*

Christ has 'summoned' the Spirit – what a vivid description. The confession as a clear-thinking vessel is filled with the Spirit. Spirit is itself absolute fullness, which breaks into the awakening human heart. The Gospel of John tells us how, at Easter, Christ

10. PENTECOST: FLAME OF SPIRIT

Jesus breathed upon his disciples and said, 'Receive the Holy Spirit' (20:22). From this first, seed-like breath of Spirit, Christ has now summoned the Spirit to flaming fullness. Our being is ignited by it, just as the plant is ignited when it blossoms. This fullness is inclined to spread and become a wildfire that ignites the hearts of all people. The grace of the original beginning is renewed: 'Out of his fullness we have all received grace in place of grace already given' (Jn 1:16).

The 'summoned' Spirit of Pentecost arrives gradually and yet, unexpectedly and suddenly. The festival period becomes a new beginning that occurs individually, in which the goals of both Easter and Ascension come to fulfilment. What seems to be an end – the fiftieth day after Easter – in fact, becomes a new beginning. This is when the work of Christ *for* human beings stands back-to-back with the work of Christ *out of* human beings, in and for the world.

The inserted prayer ends with an expansive promise for the future. A comprehensive, holistic perspective of the healing of human beings emerges from the Spirit. The I experiences healing from on high, and, healed by the Spirit, it now has the task of permeating and healing the other parts of its own being. Pentecost is the true salutogenesis – the origin of health – of the future, the spiritual fount of healing. The healing spirit begins in the comprehensive consciousness, ignites our hearts and works as a 'world-physician' right into our etheric and bodily constitution to make it whole again.

> *That healed by the Spirit*
> *Human souls*
> *Keep themselves whole*
> *Through all earthly cycles of time.*

The eternal Pentecost is the fountain of salvation for human beings.

Explanatory notes

On the occasion of Rudolf Steiner's last Pentecost on earth, he gave the lecture entitled, 'The Whitsuntide Festival: its Place in the Study of Karma,' in which he linked Christmas, Easter and Pentecost with the Rosicrucian meditation:

> The Christmas thought: *Ex deo nascimur;*
> The Easter thought: *In Christo morimur;*
> The Pentecost thought: *Per spiritum sanctum reviviscimus.*

He also explained how these festivals are directly related to the starry world:

> The language of the stars speaks to us through the thoughts of Christmas, Easter and Whitsuntide; from the Christmas thought, inasmuch as the earth is a star within the universe; through the Easter thought inasmuch as the most radiant of stars, the sun, gives us its gifts of grace; and through the Whitsun thought inasmuch as that which lies hidden beyond the stars shines into the soul, and shines forth again from the soul in the fiery tongues of Pentecost.[2]

Similarly, the inserted prayer states that the 'flames stream heavenward' and – like an echo – 'stream forth from human hearts'.

11. St John's Tide

Christ's Light in the Light of Day

St John's Tide is a time of thanksgiving. The sacramental archetype of thanksgiving is embodied in the Lord's Supper, where Christ takes hold of the substances of the earth, lifts them up and turns to the heavenly Father – 'thanking you, and uniting his soul therewith'. Thanksgiving connects him with the Ground of all Being. That is why we also call the Holy Communion 'Eucharist', which stems from the Greek word for 'giving thanks'. We hear this theme of thanksgiving at the beginning of the St John's Tide epistle. It calls us to allow abundance, gratitude and expansiveness to flow out of our souls. Practising gratitude is one of the basic elements of self-education today; it creates an important counterweight to the modern addiction to criticism. The mother of gratitude is wonder, and the sacrament provides a chance to cultivate this anew each time we attend.

Wonder begins with a conscious pause in the midst of the frenetic rush that we invariably feel afflicted with nowadays. When we consciously pause, we slow time down from a rushing brook to a broad river. Time contracts when something appeals to us or astonishes us. The decisive factor is whether we notice this – whether we can be attentive to it and enter the silence of condensed, warmed presence that comprises this moment of still awe. Genuine wonder creates an inviting space in which deep happiness and gratitude can arise, which can in turn lead to feeling honoured to participate in the inside of existence, the intimacy of original creation. Our life is constantly nourished by the love-filled power and workings of the Father.

'My heart thanks that my eye can see'.[1] This children's prayer by Rudolf Steiner breathes a John's Tide mood. The sensory world becomes translucent in our eyes. We sense the sustaining goodness of God the Father in everything that surrounds us and we respond with astonished gratitude, intimating the truth of *Ex deo nascimur,* 'We are born out of God'.

> *To the Father God*
> *All-wielding*
> *All-blessing*
> *Shall stream*
> *Our souls' devoted*
> *And heart-warm thanks.*

Our gaze is directed towards the overflowing light that shines through our world, and we are guided to perceive the inner qualities of light through the outside. To our gratitude-filled eyes, the world appears in a new guise. In the Epiphany season we heard about the light of grace – Christ's 'grace-appearance of the world's light'. During St John's Tide, we are led into the 'ether-spaces' in which the spiritual world and the sensory world touch and permeate each other.[2] With this new ability to see, practised through our experience of Christ's light, we can now recognise the grace-radiating quality of the light of St John.

> *In ether-spaces, radiant with grace, light of worlds*
> *Works in fullness, in ripening glory*
> *The Father God's all-wielding power*
> *The Father God's all-blessing might*
> *They work in the flowing ether-light*

The sun reveals its inner quality in three ways. The all-encompassing 'light of worlds' goes beyond all spatial dimensions; new worlds open up in the light and through the light. Through

11. ST JOHN'S TIDE: CHRIST'S LIGHT IN THE LIGHT OF DAY

this light, we can experience God the Father – as light from uncreated light – in his active strength and blessing power. Coming from the 'flowing ether-light', our St John's Tide gaze focuses as if through a lens and discovers the divine working of light as a second quality in the creating world of beings: the forces that conjure up from earthly substances everything that grows have been creating in the world since the beginning.

They create in the living world of being

Now, however, a third quality is added. The divine Father world forms a centre for a *cosmic rebirth*. The Son born in eternity is born anew out of the Father's powers of blessing. The creative and blessing-bestowing powers of the Father.

They ripen in the midst of the world
Into the Christ-Sun that saves mankind.

We experience the cosmic birth of light of the Son's sun from the all-embracing Father-Ground, the sunrise from the heights, the ripening of the Christ-Sun. From the cosmic birth of the Christ-Sun we are led to the incarnation of the Sun-Spirit in the earthly world. Only as a human being can Christ redeem humanity. The 'Sun-Spirit' brings it to light:

In the Sun-Spirit's ether rays
You, our Deliverer, entered
The guilt-laden seed of humanity, needy of healing
On the field of earth.

From a divine perspective, humanity appears as a seed sown by a divine hand. 'A farmer went out to sow his seed' (Lk 8:5). Golden seed of heaven is the core of our humanity; we were sown into the field of earth as human seed. John the Baptist is the great helper of humanity on the path from seed to the fruit of the spirit. (St John's Tide is the only Christian festival season to carry the name of a human being.) A 'guilt-laden' humanity is in need of healing and help in order to fulfil its mission on earth, namely the creation of the New Jerusalem.

> *And humbly bearing*
> *The Father-Spirit*
> *In the sphere around his body*
>   *I o a n e s*
> *He spoke the word of annunciation*
> *The health-bearing, guilt-conscious*
>   *Word of flame*

John the Baptist represents the culmination of prophethood, and as such is a beacon of consciousness in human evolution. During St John's Tide we participate in his consciousness open to the spirit that reaches the angelic world of the Father God.

It is in the 'not-I' activity that the I truly becomes capable of God, an attitude embodied by St Paul (Gal 2:20). This can be heard as an echo of John the Baptist's 'I am not' when asked if he was the Messiah (Jn 1:20). Just as the great task of John the Baptist was to pave the way for the incarnation of Christ Jesus, today he paves the way for the power of the Risen Christ to work in our present world. As the midwife of Christ-consciousness, John shows us the meaning of this festive season. He takes our souls into a great upsurge, quickening our consciousness.

We are surrounded by the spiritual world – 'The kingdom of God has come near' (Mk 1:15) – but can we expand our consciousness to the point where this realm of activity becomes apparent to us? John the Baptist's word of flame – 'Repent' as it is usually translated – is essentially a call to 'Change your hearts and minds' (Mk 1:15), for it is from that world that we receive decisive impulses for the becoming of the world. In the devotional mood of St John's Tide, we reach out to the sphere of morality, to the realm of the Archai – the servants of Christ who order and direct the 'advancement of the world', as we hear it in the Creed.

11. ST JOHN'S TIDE: CHRIST'S LIGHT IN THE LIGHT OF DAY

The St John's Tide Act of Consecration is a healing balm for our Christ-sense. Through the festive prayers we turn to St John as the angel of knowing, as it were. Through his humility and modesty we can learn to 'change our hearts and minds' and awaken to Christ. Instead of 'You are Christ,' we could say, 'You are the sun.' Christ is the God of the sun and the God of the human being. In an unprecedented way, he reconnects the kingdoms of heaven and earth, which were separate but belong together.

Christ entered the earth world in the rays of the spiritual sun that makes all life on earth possible. Christ, the high sun-being, is 'the heart of God', (a phrase Jakob Boehme and William Blake used) and humanity on earth is receiving a new heart: the Christ-sun-heart begins to beat within humanity. But has anyone understood that Christ united with the earth on the spiritual rays of the sun, that he took the earth cosmically into his arms? Has anyone grasped this today?

John the Baptist is the great human messenger of the gods: his spiritual-soul nature extended far beyond his physical body, making an immediate closeness to God possible for him at a time when the spiritual-soul nature of humanity was contracting. This closeness to God enabled him to awaken a consciousness of the self in earthly human beings. This closeness kindled his mission to prophecy with his spirit-filled word of flame. He sensed that human beings – endangered and embattled down to they physical body as they were – should experience salvation.

In the grace of death and resurrection, the meaning of the earth was revealed anew: the new Adam, who develops and unites freedom and love. Celebrating St John's Tide means to feel the meaning of the earth in ourselves and to want to realise it. Every true prayer along the lines of 'Your will be done' is a step on the path, and at the destination of the path, in the distant future, we will be allowed to live 'in pure ether-spheres'.

> *His grace-divining*
> *Word of flame*
> *May it burn in our hearts*
> *Longing for you,*
> *Who for us guilty human beings*
> *Have born life from death*
> *That we may live*
> *In pure ether-spheres*
> *Which can bear the guiltless alone*
> *On the glancing waves of spirit.*

In his consciousness, John reaches back to Adam, who, as the original human seed, owes his existence to the divine will. And now he shows us the path of light far into the future. As a herald of light, John has risen in the darkness of the present time on earth, filled with longing for the light of Christ. This longing opens his inner eye so that he can recognise the one who lives, works and blesses in the light: the Light-Giver and Light-Creator. The grace of knowledge now experiences the activity of the grace of God in the light:

> *He who longs for the light*
> *Who knows the light*
> *Reveals to our souls*
> *Light's radiance of grace*

In this way, John guides us through a purification process that leads us back to our essence. Integral to this process is the awareness of guilt, but also a deep 'longing for you', as the epistle states, namely for the one who has – for our sake – given birth to new life out of death.

The whole panorama of human history appears before our inner gaze. Our inner sense for Christ and for his deeds grows as we open ourselves to the proclamation of John the Baptist. He awakens in us the love for Christ and the longing for union with him:

11. ST JOHN'S TIDE: CHRIST'S LIGHT IN THE LIGHT OF DAY

> *May our soul receive*
> *The bestower of light*
> *The creator of light*
> *In light's fullness of love.*

The inserted prayer for St John's Tide is only heard after the Offertory. Having become deeply connected with him through our own endeavours during the sacrament, we turn to St John as the genius of transformation:

> *Aflame with the light of the sun*
> *Devoted to the light of worlds*
> *You, humbly bearing*
> *The Father-Spirit*
> *In the sphere around your body*
>   *I o a n e s*
> *Herald of salvation*

We ask him for his presence in the sacrament, for his awake and worldly view of the 'deed of the altar', which in our dimension becomes an act of blessing for humanity. We human beings are hereby allowed to contribute to creating the future. Through Christ's blessing we are made worthy to participate in the salvation of the world that takes place at the altar, for under the gaze of John the event at the altar becomes a true world event.

> *Look upon the deed of the altar*
> *Which blesses human beings*
> *Which we would fulfill*
> *Through the blessing of Christ*
> *Announced to us*
> *In you.*

Explanatory notes

There is an important reference to gratitude and its fundamental meaning in Rudolf Steiner's book *How to Know Higher Worlds.* This passage describes how the 'all-embracing love' that arises from gratitude is a prerequisite for knowledge. Gratitude is therefore a requirement of esoteric training:

> The sixth requirement is that we develop the feeling of gratitude for all that we receive. We should know that our very existence is a gift from the whole universe. How much is necessary for human beings to receive and sustain their existence! We owe so much to nature and to other people. Grateful thoughts such as these must become second nature for those engaged in esoteric training. If we do not give ourselves fully to such thoughts, we shall never develop the *all-embracing love* that we need to attain higher knowledge. Only if I love something can it reveal itself to me. And every revelation should fill me with thankfulness, for I am made richer by it.[3]

We hear an echo of this in the epistle: 'To the Father God ... shall stream our souls' devoted and heart-warm thanks'.

St John's Tide is related to time in a special way. John the Baptist is the spirit of the turning point of time: the time of new closeness to God – the kingdom of heaven – has come near. Time has been fulfilled. Looking up to the spiritual sun, time can be experienced anew. According to Rudolf Steiner:

> Then we shall look up to the sun and say to ourselves: 'As I look up to the sun I must behold in the sunshine the realm of time, which is hidden to the world of space. Within the sun is time; and from the realm of time that weaves within the sun Christ came forth into space, came to the earth.'

11. ST JOHN'S TIDE: CHRIST'S LIGHT IN THE LIGHT OF DAY

> ... When we look up from the earth to the sun, we are at the same time looking into the *flow of time*.[4]

We see the sun in a spiritual way when we forget about space and pay attention only to time. The sun is an 'extraordinary star' because we look out beyond space. Considering the sun's relationship to time reveals a momentous truth: 'Christ ... brought the element of time to humanity.' According to Rudolf Steiner, this was a direct message from Christ to his closest circle of disciples:

> To his intimate disciples Christ spoke these words: 'Behold the life of the earth; it is related to the life of the cosmos. When you look out on the earth and the surrounding cosmos, it is the Father whose life permeates this universe. The Father-God is the God of space. But I make known to you that I have come to you from the sun, from time – time that receives man only when he dies. I have brought you myself from the realm of time. If you receive me, you receive time, and you will not be held spellbound in space.'

Festivals in ancient times were orientated around the course of the sun, so that the peak of the festive year was reached when the sun was at its zenith. In large folk festivals, people came together to do circle dances, and the rhythm of the accompanying instruments and songs brought the souls into an ecstatic mood. In this dreamlike consciousness they gave themselves completely over to the sun element. For them, the sun was not only an outer star, but an all-encompassing deity. It was as if the window of heaven opened up for the celebrating people in their dreamlike state. They dreamt their I, but at the same time realised that their higher self was safe and protected in the heavens.

The festivals gave people the opportunity to look upwards, and also gave them the feeling that their I actually lives in the bosom of the sun, in the realm of the gods. The realisation dawned that the realm of the spiritual sun is our actual home. An echo and reflection of this ecstatic summer dream accompanied the people into the autumn. They had received the light and seen their own essence in the being that reigns in that light, and how that essence has its home in the heavens. The meaning of the great summer festivals was: *Receive wisdom in the light.*

The message of John the Baptist was: this kingdom has come near. It has become attainable for every earthly human self if we change our hearts and minds.

12. Michaelmas

The Heart's Journey to Christ

The divine reveals itself to human beings in different ways – in nature, in the progression of human history, and in the life of the individual. With the Michaelmas epistle we hear about the spiritual being who is the spirit of the age. Without mentioning his name, the epistle characterises the archangel Michael in many different ways, standing in the stream of time between the past and the present.[1] From these qualitative descriptions the image of his being can arise in our soul and become experience.

'The eyes of our souls behold ...' This is how the epistle begins, expressing as a fact what we are perhaps not even aware of yet. Can we perceive something without realising it? Then it becomes a question of extending our attention into new spiritual territory. With the foundation of all the other revelations from Christmas through St John's Tide, we now become aware of the 'eyes of our soul' and their ability to see, out of which grows a sense of responsibility to nurture these new perceptions.

> *The eyes of our souls behold,*
> *While in this hour from the altar*
> *We are to experience in our heart*
> *The consecrating of the human being:*
> *The countenance of him, who is himself*
> *The countenance of the God of our humanity.*

Spiritual vision begins with the experience of being looked at. Michael, the face of Christ, is looking at us. In Michael, Christ becomes a manifest image for us, an invisible yet visible counterpart. Michael's nature is perfect selflessness: his attitude towards Christ is one of complete devotion, so that through Michael's face we see the face of Christ himself looking at us.

Can I face this? Am I ready and willing to be looked at? In this back and forth of looking and being looked at, the human world and the divine world draw nearer to each other. A sacramental consciousness is formed in which clarity of thought and spiritual experience interweave. What emanates from the event at the altar, which we can experience in our hearts as a consecrating force, is the foundation from which we experience everything else.

In connection with the Michaelmas epistle, the 'sense for the I' is of particular importance. This does not refer, as one might think, to the perception of one's own self, but rather the perception of the I of the *other*. We could therefore also call it the 'sense for you'.[2] This sense is not limited to the human world, however; the beings of the higher hierarchies also have an I quality.

We also use 'you' in praying to the divine Trinity, which belies an implicit truth regarding the existence of the Father, the Son and the Holy Spirit – otherwise we would be using empty formulas in our prayers. Is an initial perception of a being not the prerequisite for addressing that being as a you? We can try to think through the following: the Michaelmas prayers speak to us of a perception of the innermost heart, which usually remains hidden to us. This implies that the words of the sacrament are words of reflection, in that they awaken our heart's ability to sense the beginnings of a hidden event that grows on us the more we learn to experience the Act of Consecration in our hearts. In the service of Christ, Michael wants to lead us into the activity of what in the epistle is called 'higher divining', in which our 'sense for the I' is activated. As a child once so aptly worded it, Michael is the heart-angel of our time.

Tracing the heart motifs in the Michaelmas epistle can reveal the golden thread of the Michael-Christ path, which leads us to the forces that overcome death within us. The point of departure

12. MICHAELMAS: THE HEART'S JOURNEY TO CHRIST

for this journey is the invitation to experience the Consecration of the Human Being in our hearts. This will free up the strength that Michael can release from human hearts. The path of heart preparation brings us face to face with the earnest countenance of Michael – and through him, leads further to the light of Christ. He sends his strength into our hearts when the longing for salvation ignites the fire of our hearts. Christ's strength or power is at the same time our free strength, which Michael can grasp when our hearts turn towards him. Michael is the guardian of this journey of the heart.

> *So stands he in these world-days,*
> *Clear shining, as Christ's countenance*
> *As guardian before the hallowed offering.*

Michael, archangel of the sun, carries brightly radiating cosmic sun forces into our earthly world in the present epoch of humanity. The spiritual power of the sun is the deepest secret of Christianity and is expressed in the following verse by Rudolf Steiner.

> Looking upwards I can see
> In the bright circle of the sun
> The mighty heart of the world.
> Looking inwards I can feel
> In the warm beat of the heart
> The ensouled human sun.[3]

The outer sun continually gives its powers to the earth: all life develops in its light and warmth. In the same way, we also need to be close to Christ in order to find in his presence the strength and affirmation through which he can develop his true nature and make fruitful everything in the world that is in the process of becoming.

The motif that now follows in the epistle is one of the most earnest that we encounter in the course of the Christian year. It has to do with beings of the spiritual hierarchies whose intentions and endeavours are directed towards binding the human spirit to the earth. They are called 'powers', and are powerful beings who have alienated themselves from their divine origin. Without help, we humans would be hopelessly at their mercy, for they have an intelligence far superior to ours. They can only work where they manage to remain unnoticed, however, and by naming them, the sacrament confronts us with their existence, while at the same time allowing us to experience Michael's victory over these forces.[4]

> *The powers that would fetter the human spirit*
> *In chains of earthly slavery*
> *He treads under his feet,*
> *Which are free of the weight of earth.*

Through this ongoing act of Michael, the space is created in which human freedom becomes possible – a freedom that at the same time implies a responsibility towards all that belongs to the earth.

Hidden in our heart lies the counterforce that can bring about the continuation of the world when heaven and earth pass away. Experiencing this free power is the second stage of the journey of the heart that we have outlined above. It also causes our thinking to become animated with the heavenly forces of truth, beauty and goodness. Michael stimulates the spiritualisation of earthly intelligence to reconnect it with its divine origin. By letting the spirit of Michael freely into our heart, we can expand beyond ourselves and resist the adversarial powers. The combination of our free power with receptivity to the spirit serves the further maturation for what is to come. The epistle puts it in monumentally simple terms: human hearts are being prepared for the light.

12. MICHAELMAS: THE HEART'S JOURNEY TO CHRIST

> *And from human hearts he brings forth*
> *The free power, which can bear the earthly*
> *Into heights of heaven, making it pure*
> *And Spirit receptive.*
> *Earnestness streams from his shining,*
> *Earnestness that before the gentleness of Christ*
> *Prepares human hearts for the light.*

From Michael's countenance radiates the revitalising power of the sun, but at the same time also purifying earnestness.[5] In this schooling of the heart, we are being prepared to receive the gentle light of Christ. Only those who have become light themselves can receive the light of Christ within their hearts.

With respect to the adversarial powers, the epistle shows us a completely new side of Michael's activity that is only being revealed today. Michael is and remains on the one hand the dragon-fighter who holds at bay the forces that threaten humanity. At the same time, however, and as the epistle says, just 'for moments', we may perceive a gesture of beckoning. The heart that is prepared for the light can perceive Michael's beckoning and follow it. The ability to think from the heart develops in the interplay between clarity of thought and sacrificial warmth, which the epistle calls 'higher divining'.

> *Whoever beheld him in years past*
> *Perceived the stern hand, threatening,*
> *Stretched toward the dragon's power.*
> *Whoever beholds him today becomes aware*
> *How for moments he changes*
> *The sternness against the power of the enemy:*
> *And forming his hand to beckon*
> *He shows us: Follow me.*
> *I lead you to the higher divining*
> *Of the deed of life and death on Golgotha ...*

This sacrifice of Christ reveals itself to the 'higher divining' as the deed of life and death on Golgotha, which is meant to continue to work towards the salvation of creation within human beings. This salvation is described in simple but great words, telling us that we are to join life with light to prevent the divine light in the earthly light from being extinguished.

> *... the deed of life and death on Golgotha,*
> *Which working on in the earthly human being*
> *Creating into times to come*
> *Shall to life bring light.*
> *That in the earthly light*
> *The heavenly light vanish not,*
> *Which is to shine as from the beginning,*
> *So now and in all cycles of time.*

Strength rings out from the words that describe the continued activity of Christ in and through us. It is in human beings that the deed of life and death on Golgotha is to continue to work and become a spiritually powerful force in the future; it is through human beings that new spiritual light is to be given to life. How will we be able to do this? How will we – mere human beings – be able to grow into the kind of activity that the divine world expects of us?

The journey of the Michaelmas epistle pauses for the Gospel and Creed. The gospel reading, Matthew 22, tells of the royal wedding. The beckoning gesture of the epistle becomes the call, 'Come to the wedding.' It was customary at that time to provide the wedding guests with a wedding garment. What is the garment being offered to us in this case? After the feeling of helplessness at the end of the epistle, we are now met with an offer of grace as if saying, 'Let divine grace clothe you! What you lack here, God can fill in there!' The crucial question is then, can I accept the helping grace or do I refuse it?

12. MICHAELMAS: THE HEART'S JOURNEY TO CHRIST

The Creed tells us that the world has been changed in its innermost aspect by the entry of Christ into the development of earth and humanity, that the divine has been given back to us, and that it is now up to us to recognise and confess it: 'Yes, so it is.' If I connect my own heart with the statements of this renewed Creed, it becomes my personal confession. The insights that the Creed introduce become the basis of a new faith – a faith that is no longer blind, but that sees. I let the Creed find its way into my heart, as the word itself suggests: *credo* means I connect my heart with the divine. Purified through powerlessness, awakened by the parable of the royal wedding, and strengthened by the panorama of knowledge that our Creed presents, the journey of the heart can continue.

The spiritual world addresses us, calling us to a way of thinking in the form of 'higher divining' and to willing in the form of future tasks. The epistle helps empower our heart in order to fulfil our future mission: to give new spiritual light to life. We are led into new territory of the soul – the region where Christ has entered in the celebration of the festivals from Advent until now. This is where the little spark can become a fire. Here we encounter Christ: he sees our weakness, but he is ready to send his 'power-bearing spirit' into our hearts so that we can fulfil our mission as human beings:

> *May he lead us into depths of soul,*
> *From which Christ sends his power*
> *Bearing spirit into human hearts*
> *When, in true longing for salvation,*
> *We feel the fire of the heart*
> *Rightly enkindled.*

If in the initial Michaelmas epistle the Easter event is reflected in the 'higher divining' of the Mystery of Golgotha, inner qualities of the Ascension and Pentecost appear in the inserted prayer. Heavenly paths and the events of Pentecost become an individual experience of the soul when a person – out of a deep longing for salvation – turns to Michael and follows his beckoning. This is the true turning point. It begins in the human heart, which becomes capable of receiving the spirit that Christ brings to it. The healing spirit kindles a fire in the human heart through which the Risen One can continue to work into the future as an inexhaustible source of spiritual strength.

> *He who stood before the Father God*
> *Who stands before the Son God*
> *To him shall our hearts turn*
> *That the healing Spirit work in us*
> *As from the beginning,*
> *So now and through all cycles of time.*

Explanatory notes

The creation of a new Michaelmas festival is part of the larger context of exploring and presenting the esoteric background of the cycle of the year. As early as March 1917, Rudolf Steiner spoke in a completely new way about the cycle of the year in terms of the task of linking the further development of Christianity with the further development of humanity. He developed the following main ideas in the lecture:

- The cosmic dimension of the Christ must be recognised.
- The cosmic dimension includes the fact that the Christ, since the mystery of Golgotha, 'belongs to the cycle of the year'.
- Experiencing the cycle of the year creates social knowledge and social feeling.
- Experiencing the cosmic Christ in the cycle of the year creates a sense of community.

12. MICHAELMAS: THE HEART'S JOURNEY TO CHRIST

He concluded with the decisive and monumental statement that experiencing Christ's activity throughout the cycle of the year prepares us for his return.[6] In a continuation of these thoughts, on the day before Christmas of the same year, Steiner stated that Christianity has connected the mysteries of the world with the cycle of the year.[7]

About two years later, Friedrich Rittelmeyer asked Rudolf Steiner about the Second Coming of Christ, specifically, what could be done to prepare for Damascus-like experiences. He received the answer, 'That is only possible if you experience Christ in the cycle of the year.'[8]

The depictions of the cycle of the year solidified at the end of 1922 and into 1923. On December 24, 1922, he spoke of the initiates of the so-called year-god and their teachings. The deep winter 'festival of sorrow and mourning' was transformed into a festival of inner, spiritual joy among those who experienced the being of Christ. Steiner then refers to the Michael-revelation that began in the last third of the nineteenth century, linking it in a new way to the entire cycle of seasons, specifically to the new experience of Christmas:

> Today is the time when the path must be found from the Michael festival to the Midwinter festival, when there should come to pass a *sunrise of the Spirit* ...
>
> If men do but try with depth and tenderness of feeling and with strongest power of will to find in the darkness the light of the Spirit, then that light will shine as did the stars of heaven when the birth of Jesus was announced to the shepherds and the magi.[9]

The idea of the creation of a new Michaelmas festival continued to run through Rudolf Steiner's lectures in 1923. Some motifs from the first half of the year are mentioned here, because they illuminate the spiritual background and at the same time shed light on the surprising handover of the Michaelmas epistle to The Christian Community on September 13, 1923.

On Easter Monday 1923, for example, the failure of the movement for threefold social order in 1919 was retrospectively associated with the lack of Michaelic force:

> One might say that when we spoke of the threefold impulse it was in a certain sense a test of whether the Michael thought is already strong enough so that it can be felt how such an impulse flows directly out of the forces that shape the time. It was a test of the human soul, of whether the Michael thought is strong enough as yet in a large number of people. Well, the test yielded a negative result. The Michael thought is not strong enough in even a small number of people for it to be perceived truly in all its time-shaping power and forcefulness.[10]

As regards the future, Steiner then said:

> And it will indeed hardly be possible, for the sake of new forces of ascent, to unite human souls with the original formative cosmic forces in the way that is necessary, unless such an inspiring force as can permeate a Michael festival – unless, that is to say, a new formative impulse – can come forth from the depths of the esoteric life.
>   If instead of the passive members of the Anthroposophical Society, even only a few active members could be found, then it would become possible to set up further deliberations to consider such a thought.

The day before, on Easter Sunday, Rudolf Steiner had already demanded 'esoteric maturity' from his listeners:

> Mankind must attain an esoteric maturity ... to be able again to think so concretely that men can again become festival-creating ...

12. MICHAELMAS: THE HEART'S JOURNEY TO CHRIST

It is not admissible today for a person merely to indulge in esoteric speculations; it is necessary today to be able once again to *do the esoteric*.[11]

Shortly after Pentecost in 1923, Rudolf Steiner gave his last lecture in Berlin, in which he again spoke insistently and at length of the necessity, but also of the enormous task to create a new Michaelmas festival.[12] He saw it as necessary that this festival be a powerful impulse for the continuation of not only our civilisation but also our whole life! This would require the strength, courage and seriousness of a number of understanding people who would be able to take seriously feeling and living into the spirit. A higher, living anthroposophy is necessary for this, for serving Michael entails reintroducing spirituality back into our actions. Michael must once again become our guiding spirit for the development of civilisation. This will be possible if we can once again in the spiritual sense connect with the cycle of the year. To grasp and live the spiritual content of the yearly cycle of festivals is to serve Michael. The creation of festivals should reveal the divine will, to which people must reconnect.

Alluding to the Goetheanum fire on New Year's Eve 1922, Steiner ends the lecture with a Pentecostal call to create festivals through true spiritual enthusiasm.

A few weeks later, the priests of The Christian Community had a meeting with Rudolf Steiner in Stuttgart from July 11 to 14, 1923. Steiner invited the leadership of the priests to a special meeting after the lecture on July 13. One of the many questions discussed related to the new Michaelmas festival, namely whether there would also be such a festival within the religious renewal movement. Rudolf Steiner waved it away: 'This year it will not yet be possible to introduce this festival as a new festival; that can only be done in connection with the advance in *Weltanschauung*.'

This made the events in September all the more surprising.

When Rudolf Steiner arrived in Stuttgart from Dornach to hold a lecture on September 13, 1923, he summoned the priests Gertrud Spörri and Emil Bock and gave them the Michaelmas texts. Steiner handed over the texts to them with radiant joy. They were almost overwhelmed by the sudden prospect of the unprecedented new content, that the festival of St Michael had now been added to the Christian year. Steiner himself was obviously also impressed by the inauguration element involved. He added: 'To begin with, you should repeat these texts until the beginning of a new festival – in other words until Advent.'[13]

It must have been revealed to Rudolf Steiner sometime between July and September 1923, that there was a living impulse in the spiritual world that would allow the inauguration of the new Michaelmas festival in the ritual sphere. This would support and advance the inner spiritual activity of human beings – both a gift of the spirit and the highest expectation at the same time.

A characteristic feature of this festival in the ritual context lies in the fact that the individual – a decisive element of the Michaelmas festival – is deeply connected with the communal: 'The eyes of *our* souls behold, while ... *we* are to experience ...' At the same time, however, Michael's call is addressed specifically to the individual, to the free human I: 'Follow me. I lead you [singular] to the higher divining ...'

Hearing this call, individuals come together and form a community in which no one retains anything for themselves. Everyone is united by the common task that approaches us from the future: to continue to shine the light of heaven on earth. The experience of the Michaelmas epistle and the Michaelmas Consecration of the Human Being can engender in the congregation the awareness and empowerment for this task, but only the individual can take up the task in their life.

The lectures about Michaelmas held in Vienna at the end of September and beginning of October 1923, can lend quite a bit of insight into the Michaelmas epistle. In the introduction Rudolf Steiner explains why – especially while being in Austria – he chooses to focus on the *Gemüt*, the German word encompassing heart and mind. He emphasises that today the *Gemüt* is once again capable of cognition and can contribute decisively to a fuller cognitive process than previously possible. Along these lines, the human being's 'eyes of the soul' are mentioned several times, which we also hear at the beginning of the epistle: 'The eyes of our souls behold'.

He describes Michael's conflict with the dragon as threefold: firstly, in a pre-human, pre-earthly time, then the historical conflict in the nineteenth century that culminates in Michael's victory in 1879, and finally, as an everlasting battle within every human being. The epistle reflects this in the threefold formulation: 'once … in years past … today'.

There are two references to seeing the spirit figure of Michael. On the one hand, Steiner states surprisingly concretely that 'we see the higher things with the back of our head'. We carry an etheric image of Michael within us. This image can be called forth through human devotion, which is how this Michael-power can at the same time be understood as our own free power, 'for it is not Michael himself who wages the battle, but human devotion and the resulting image of Michael … The radiant figure of Michael may stand before the soul's eye – radiant in spiritual vision, yet within the reach of ordinary consciousness.' Again, we hear an echo of the epistle's words, 'The eyes of our souls behold'.

At the end of this lecture, given two days before Michaelmas, Rudolf Steiner addresses his listeners with a rousing, solemn charge, telling of a new alliance with Michael:

> If the requisite goodwill were forthcoming in extensive circles to raise such a conception to a religious force and to inscribe it in every *Gemüt* … we would have something that once again could seize hold on the whole inner man, because that is what can be inscribed in that living *Gemüt* … The striving for enlightenment would become inwardly and deeply religious … This will regain its significance only when we are able to experience in our soul such a living vision.[14]

A few days later, the Michaelmas epistle is heard at the altars for the first time. The inner heartfelt teachings of Michael are revealed once again: 'The eyes of our souls behold'.

The question can arise as to whether Michael really stood before the Father God, or before Yahweh, the god of the Israelite people. Rudolf Steiner gave an interesting answer to this question in his last Easter lecture about the mystery centre of Ephesus, and mentions Jehovah in that context.

Everything in Ephesus was oriented towards experiencing the way the spirit lives and weaves within the ether of the world, in joy over all that bears fruit, over all that sprouts and grows. J O A resounded here from out of the cosmos (the J is pronounced Y in English):

> 'J O' equalled the ego and astral body, and they perceived the approach of the etheric light-body in the 'A', forming together 'J O A' ...
>
> Then it was as if there rang forth from the earth (for we were now entered into the cosmos) something which enforced the 'J O A', making of it 'eh v', 'JehOvA'. It was the forces of the earth that revealed themselves in the 'eh v'.
>
> The neophyte now felt his whole human being in the 'JehOvA'. He felt a premonition of the physical body as it was first on earth in the consonants which accompanied the vocalisation, which in the 'J O A' indicated the ego, the astral body, and the etheric body.[15]

In this way, the disciple undergoing initiation at Ephesus lived into the final steps that every human being goes through when descending from the spiritual world into a human body. Michael, the archangel of the sun, works into the sphere of the moon, in which the prenatal human being is formed out of the Fatherly forces of the world: *ex Deo nascimur*. From this point of view, Michael is not only the spirit of the Israelite people, but is also involved in the formation of the human body in general, and especially in that of the human god, the Son of Man, who was sent by God the Father.

The fact that it is justified to speak of Michael having once stood before the Father God is also evident from another statement by Rudolf Steiner, where he describes the Israelite religion, led on the level of the folk spirits by Michael, as a 'Father religion':

> It is the essential characteristic of a Moon religion, a religion like that of the ancient Hebrews, in which the Father principle is predominant, always to attach value in the human being only to what has been bestowed upon him through the forces of the Father God, through the Moon forces.[16]

As for the malicious spirits that want to 'fetter the human spirit in chains of earthly slavery', Rudolf Steiner gives his listeners an unsparing account of what the consequences would be in the future if people only engaged in 'automatic, lifeless thoughts'. The entirety of humanity would withdraw from the earth; such erroneous thoughts could lead to the creation of a world full of evil, destructive beings.

> All the beings presently conceived so incorrectly in people's thoughts – incorrectly because the mere shadowy intellect can only conceive of the mineral, the crudely material element, be it in the mineral, plant, animal or even human kingdom – these thoughts of human beings that have no reality all of a sudden will become realities when the moon and the earth unite again. From the earth, there will spring forth a horrible brood of beings. In character they will be between the mineral and the plant kingdoms. They will be beings resembling automatons, with an overabundant intellect of great intensity. Along with this development, which will spread over the earth, the latter will be covered as if by a network or web of ghastly spiders possessing tremendous wisdom. Yet their organisation will not even

reach up to the level of the plants. They will be horrible spiders who will be entangled with one another. In their outward movements they will imitate everything human beings have thought up with their shadowy intellect, which did not allow itself to be stimulated by what is to come through new imagination and through spiritual science in general.

All these unreal thoughts people are thinking will be endowed with being. As it is covered by layers of air today, or occasionally with swarms of locusts, the earth will be covered with hideous mineral-plant-like spiders that intertwine with one another most cleverly but in a frighteningly evil manner. To the extent that human beings have not enlivened their shadowy, intellectual concepts, they will have to unite their being, not with the entities who are seeking to descend since the last third of the nineteenth century, but instead with these ghastly mineral-plant-like spidery creatures.[17]

The power to seize the thoughts individually and to revitalise them from within arises in the connection with Michael. In this way, we can ally ourselves with Michael against the forces that, as we hear in the epistle, want to 'fetter the human spirit in chains of earthly slavery'.

The training of the intellect was necessary for the acquisition of freedom, but at the same time, it strengthened egoism. The path of the heart is the path to the universal human – the path not of denial, but of the overcoming of intellectualism.

Through the brain men are essentially egotistic, through the heart they become free from egoism and rise to the level of the universal-human. Thus through the sun we are more than we should be if we were left to our own resources in our present earth existence. Let me put it like this: if we can really find our way to the Christ, he enables

12. MICHAELMAS: THE HEART'S JOURNEY TO CHRIST

us, because he is a sun being, to be more than we could otherwise be.[18]

In the course of the year, Michaelmas stands opposite Easter in its timing. It is the festival of inner resurrection, when we celebrate the inner empowerment of the spirit that does not fear death. The spiritual year has produced its inner fruit. The eyes of our soul begin to see. What has already happened is now being made conscious within us; with Michaelmas, we are entrusted with this new awareness for our own further fulfilment and development. The conscious path of the heart to Christ is the cultivation of this seed, which we carry as strength into the coming year.

And what you think has happened,
Can only be seen coming from afar.

Novalis, *Heinrich von Ofterdingen,* Part 2

13.

Veins of Gold

When the blood of Christ flowed to the earth on Golgotha, it was thoroughly imbued with spiritual power. Human blood had become a pure carrier of divine ego power. In the veins of his blood lived the readiness for the great sacrificial service to the earth and humanity. In the burial of his body on Golgotha, the earth received his blood like a cosmic communion, and was permeated by the powers that had until that moment been bound in physical body and blood. That was the moment the earth became his body.

Since then, his lifelines have secretly run through all earthly things. Not in specific places, but rather, in the spaces between, and in inconspicuous moments, inconspicuous places. Everywhere, and at the same time nowhere, we find traces of his work like veins of gold.

When gold is found in the dark rock underground, we speak of 'veins of gold'. This image is taken from the realm of the living, for ordinarily veins are the blood vessels in humans and animals, or the vessels running through plant leaves. They are the pathways of life that run through matter; fine branches that enable life to permeate the organism. In the mineral world, they are usually found between two layers of rock – at the boundaries of the layers, in the void. Because such veins are small and inconspicuous, their discovery in the dark interior of the earth causes great wonder.

It is a memory of cosmic light, but also an experience in the present: matter can be illuminated in such a way that it bears witness to the light of the spirit and its all-permeating power. In the face of such a discovery, we can inwardly feel something like a small sunrise. The discovery of these sun forces hidden in the darkness comforts us – we breathe a sigh of relief at finding this bridge to the everlasting light. Running inconspicuously throughout our earthly life are such veins of light: the cosmic sun power of Christ's work.

The Act of Consecration of the Human Being serves as a vessel in time for the life currents of Christ since the event on Golgotha. It captures that which usually permeates our earthly existence so inconspicuously and which we so easily overlook. Attending the service is a chance for us to stop for a while, pause, and inhale the power of these life currents – then let them flow anew and intensified into the world so that they can in turn permeate our world like fine veins of gold: bright, warm, and heartfelt.

What is expressed in the epistles is the lifeblood of the present Christ, his cohabitation with us, his living work. The epistles therefore light up various pathways to walk with Christ: they are like veins of gold for our human life. Those who immerse themselves in their dynamics and impulses can participate in his life, developing organs to perceive his cohabitation in our earthly existence. In their trajectory throughout the cycle of the year, the epistles allow us to discover the veins of gold of his work in the organism of our revitalised earth.

Contemplations on the Epistles

Rudolf Frieling

The following contemplations were written for the priests of The Christian Community in their monthly circular (Rundbrief).

On the seasonal prayers (1926)

At the risk of stating the obvious, if we disregard the Trinity epistle, which, after all, has a more timeless character, we have exactly twelve epistles: Advent, Christmas night, dawn, and morning, Epiphany, Passiontide, Holy Week, Easter, Ascension, Pentecost, St John's Tide and Michaelmas. The structure of some of the prayers particularly caught my eye. Michaelmas and St John's Tide, for example, are especially clear in their sevenfoldness. Feeling our way into the inner sense of such a structure makes it easier to celebrate these prayers, particularly those that we see as long.

Firstly, Michaelmas. This epistle is composed of seven sentences that begin with the following phrases:

1) *The eyes of our souls ...*
2) *So stood he ...*
3) *So stands he ...*
4) *The powers ...*
5) *Earnestness ...*
6) *Whoever beheld him ...*
7) *Whoever beholds him today ...*

The centrepiece, 'The powers', represents the victory over Ahriman (*chains of earthly slavery*) and over Lucifer (*the earthly into heights of heaven*) through the 'free power' of the human heart. We can see a clear correspondence between 'So stands he' and 'Earnestness ...' (3 & 5): 'Clear shining ... as guardian ...' and 'Earnestness streams from his shining'. Likewise, between 'So stood he ...' and 'Whoever beheld him ...' (2 & 6). Finally, also between 'The eyes of our souls behold ...' and 'Whoever beholds him today ...' (1 & 7). The word 'altar' in 1 is unfolded in 7, where we hear of the primordial altar, Golgotha. Likewise, the word 'countenance of the God of our humanity' (*Menschengott*) finds an echo in the last lines about the deed of Golgotha 'working on in the earthly human being'. Finally, the immediacy of 'in this hour' (in 1) expands into 'all cycles of time' (in 7). This speaks of the overcoming of temporality, which we also see in the decay of the natural world during autumn!

St John's Tide's seven sections begin with the following words:

1) *To the Father God ...*
2) *In ether spaces ...*
3) *In the Sun-Spirit's ether rays ...*
4) *And humbly bearing the Father-Spirit ... I o a n e s ...*
5) *His grace-divining word of flame ...*
6) *He who longs for the light ...*
7) *May our soul receive ...*

Note that the centrepiece (4) puts St John in the spotlight by naming him.

The extent to which this 'passes through' the seven sheathes of our being will be easily felt by everyone.

Von Skerst[1] drew my attention to this structure. Here the arrangement alone ... [rest of line illegible] ... prayers have a clear fourfold structure, corresponding to the Consecration of the Human Being.

Clearly at Epiphany:

1) *Out of world-wide spaces appeared the star of grace:* Gospel
2) *Into the light of grace ... our souls devoted ... in humility:* Offertory
3) *May the holy Act of Consecration be fulfilled:* Transubstantiation
4) *May the heart's light of our prayer meet yearningly the world-light of the star of grace:* Communion

Von Skerst also drew my attention to the fact that these four elements can also be found in the Easter inserted prayer 'Jubilating ...':

1) The first three sentences: Gospel
2) *We find in the delight of our devoted souls:* Offertory
3) *Living is the soul which was dead:* Transubstantiation
4) *The grave of the soul opens:* Communion

Act of Consecration for One who has Died:

1) *With the word ...:* Gospel
2) *With the sacrifice ....:* Offertory
3) *Let him shine ...:* Transubstantiation
4) *Receive him ...:* Communion

The three Christmas services clearly have a relationship to the Trinity: the Spirit, Son (word), and Father (body).

The Passion texts, by contrast, are quite taciturn; they each have just five short sentences.

One can have a strange feeling of fatefulness if we consider how Dr Steiner gave the epistles in a piecemeal fashion, and how this organism of the Consecration of the Human Being was completed only just before his death.

The basic epistle (1963)

Together with the inserted prayers, the epistles form a world of their own. They only began to be added to the Act of Consecration in September 1922, beginning with the Trinity text. This Trinity prayer takes the middle ground between the main parts (as direct prayer) and the Creed (statement in the third person). The Father-Son-Spirit content of the epistle echoes the Creed, but it differs in that the first person is introduced here through the terms 'we'/'our'. One could argue, however, that the first person is implicit in the speaking of the Creed: the 'we feel' statement of the epistle's first line is akin to the Latin *credo* (I believe) or the Greek *pisteuomen* (we believe) of the Nicene Creed.

The first verse is most similar to the Creed in that it is the most conceptual (with words such as 'consciousness', 'substance', 'being', 'existence'), whereas the second stanza is more a description of experience. The third is characterised by the open future, with the use of the subjunctive coming closer to prayer as we usually think of it.

The 'we' that speaks there (just as in the opening sentence of the whole sacrament), is probably the overarching 'we' of The Christian Community. This 'we' speaks in – almost – all epistles, carrying the contemplation either intellectually, experientially or in a prayerful way of hope.

An exception is only in the spring–autumn axis. At Michaelmas, the contemplation of the figure of Michael rises to a climax, so that Michael's authoritative words become audible. This message that we receive there does not, however, have the 'we' of the community as its addressee, but pierces right through to the individual by addressing us – like the guardian of the threshold would – very intimately and personally. 'Follow me! I will lead you ...' (the singular). Apart from the peace greeting during Communion, the individual is not addressed in the entire sacrament, except in this Michael epistle and in the 'opposite' festival. Opposite Michaelmas in the cycle of the year are Passiontide, Holy Week, and Easter, and like variations on an archetypal figure, their epistles correspond sentence for sentence to the Michaelmas epistle.

The Trinity epistle (1974)

The Trinity Epistle was first introduced to us on September 8, 1922, when Rudolf Steiner demonstrated the Act of Consecration of the Human Being. In Rudolf Steiner's manuscript there is an addition: 'At the end: repeat the epistle of the beginning at the right-hand side of the altar.' The repetition at the end and on the right-hand side is explicitly stated here. In the manuscripts, the corresponding seasonal texts are without exception all titled 'epistles'.

In the Ascension epistle, we encounter for the first time the use of a future-oriented phrase: 'We would fulfil the Act of Consecration'. I remember wondering at the time whether this would also be the corresponding phrase at the end. In the original manuscript, however, there is an explicit addition to the Ascension text: 'In the same framework and in the place of the grad.' This abbreviation refers to 'gradual', which was a prayer in the Catholic mass that was spoken softly between priest and server at the beginning of the service. Rudolf Steiner obviously uses the word 'gradual' to refer to the Trinity epistle here, and what applies to the gradual, namely that it is repeated at the end, therefore also applies to the Ascension epistle.

The 'we would fulfil' at the end can thus be understood to mean that during Ascension, looking up to the exalted one, a kind of permanent, ongoing will is born – a will to participate in this continuous celebration.

At the beginning of the Michaelmas epistle, when we hear 'in this hour ... we are to experience,' then 'this hour' also applies to the entire sacramental text that follows until we hear the words 'thus it has been'.

Based on the indications given to us, we can therefore say for certain that during the festival periods, we are to read the relevant epistle in place of the Trinity text. This can also benefit our experience of the Trinity text, as we can understand it as being seasonally neutral. With each festival, its tranquil balance is altered in favour of the relevant festive content. Each festival brings an accent, and therefore a certain one-sidedness, to the sacrament. One after the other, different aspects of the overall Christian truth come to the fore.

Likewise, a new impact can be felt at the beginning of each archangel quarter. Gabriel's quarter is from Advent to Epiphany; Raphael rules the quarter from Passion to Pentecost (the longest epistle cycle); Uriel oversees the St John's text; and Michael, of course, Michaelmas. The Trinity epistle is also spoken each quarter, bringing its balancing quality. Only between 'Raphael' and 'Uriel' is this breathing room occasionally very short, to the point of not existing at all. Normally, however, we experience the lavender-hued Trinity sacrament at four different times in the year. That would then constitute the equivalent of the 'non-festival half' of the year for us, except that it would not have the negative connotation that 'non' usually does; it would simply mean that every time the specific nature of the new quarter is expressed in its (justified) one-sidedness, the Trinity overview is re-established as the comprehensive, balanced *theologia*.

We rediscover it anew each time, insofar as it has a different sound to us depending on the festival we have just finished celebrating. Our Trinity text need not suffer from being set aside during the festival periods; it can, in fact, benefit precisely from this, by being heard anew each time.

Passiontide (1963)

'O human soul' – no one addresses another person like this anymore; the 'O' expresses far too much pathos for our age. Its appearance in our age of the consciousness soul thus implies a special inner necessity. This dramatic call comes together with the shock of the black colour. The Catholic Church has a longer Passiontide, but does not impose the black colour on its believers. Black is reserved for only Good Friday and Holy Saturday – otherwise the robes are purple, which they consider a penitential colour. Our four weeks in black are a novelty.

Just like at Michaelmas, we hear ourselves addressed by a concrete being in a manner reminiscent of the strict guardian of the threshold. The 'O' gives the words 'human soul' something like a divine emotional aura, expressing a *divine* pathos as if divine beings are making us into their religion. It is as if the creative powers are now looking towards us alienated and miserable creatures.

By way of a diagnosis ('Where does it hurt?'), we are made aware of what loss we are really suffering from, and what we truly long for in the depths of our being. This diagnosis opens up the Raphael path, which then culminates with the 'world-physician' at Pentecost.

When we are spoken to regarding the head or heart, where we invariably feel something is missing, we cannot help but feel seen through and through. This piercing experience of being seen is then followed by an answer, which we hear in the epistle between the Gospel and the Offertory, and which, as if it could not begin in any other way, begins with 'Look ... not ... Look ...' Then, there appears a word that has never been uttered at a Christian altar in this form: 'My self'.

It can be strangely moving to come across a passage in Plato where he speaks of the 'sting' of evil in quite the same sense as our epistle. In his later work *Laws,* which contains many echoes of the original revelation, Plato reflects on how to deal with an evildoer who has committed crimes of the 'difficult to heal' (*dys-iata*) or even 'incurable' (*an-iata*) kind, such as robbing a temple. In this case, one must take into account 'the weakness of human nature as a whole' as a precautionary measure (*Laws,* IX. 854). Plato imagines that to a person 'whom an evil desire (*epithymia kakē*) urges during the day and at night wakes him from sleep, driving him to rob some sacred object', one would have to say the following: 'You marvellous one, that is no common human nor any divine quality that drives you to go and desecrate the temple now. It is a pernicious thorn (*oistros*) that is driving you, against which you must guard yourself with all your strength. It is implanted in people due to long ago (*palaiōn*) and still unpunished (*akathartōn*) wrongdoings.' He is instructed to visit the altars of the gods who ward off evil (*apotropaiōn*) and to keep to the community of good people. If all this does not help, he should consider that death is better, and thus, depart from life.

With such realism and deadly seriousness, long before the Mystery of Golgotha, Plato spoke of the total weakness of human nature (*sympasa tēs anthropinēs physeōs astheneia*) and of the sting that is active in human beings from times long past, inciting them to commit acts that are 'difficult to heal', or even 'incurable'.

Easter (1963)

We have seen that Plato was already writing about evil using the precise words 'sting' and 'thorn'. That brings to mind words of Steiner spoken in the lecture on March 16, 1923: 'The feeling of having lost an ancient knowledge ... most certainly weighed upon the more profound Greek souls.'[2]

At the beginning of February 1923, we received the Passion and Easter epistles together. Not long afterwards, at Easter 1923, the lecture series on the cycle of the year was held, in which we heard about the breathing of the earth. The words in the Easter inserted prayer 'breath of the earth' and the 'the spirit-radiant power of the sun' are illustrated there in a blackboard drawing.[3]

What Steiner spoke of in that lecture of March 16 can remind us of the ritual texts that had been handed over a few weeks earlier. In that lecture, he explained how our musical experience of the intervals has developed throughout the history of consciousness. Only after the human soul was completely embodied did we begin to experience the third in its fullness, including the difference between major and minor. Before that, human beings found full satisfaction in the fifth, which, far from being empty, was full of divine life. In Atlantis, the seventh was the decisive interval. It brought the souls out of their bodies and transferred them to the realm of the gods. This happened to an even greater extent in Lemuria through the octave, and even the ninth and tenth. What is significant about the tenth is that it includes the third on a new level, bringing the major and minor with it. With the interval of the tenth, this is not the third we are familiar with, in whose major and minor one hears the joy and suffering of the incarnated human being. In the Lemurian period it was the third beyond the octave, and thus major and minor beyond the octave in the macrocosmic style of the gods. Steiner calls it a kind of objective third: 'A kind of objective major and objective minor ... as the expression of the spiritual experience of the gods ... the cosmic jubilant sounds of the gods and the cosmic lamentations of the gods.' The 'jubilant music' was the expression of the 'joy over their world creation', whereas the Lemurian equivalent of our inner experience of the minor third today was that of the immense lamentation of the gods: the 'cosmic lament' over humanity's apostasy.

Today, contemporaries shake their heads when they read of the tenacity and fervour with which audiences used to listen to the ritual lamentations performed in honour of Osiris, Tammuz, Adonis or Baldur. One is tempted to think of it just as a ceremonial make-believe, where they only pretended to grieve without actually plunging themselves into that abyss of the soul. Hamlet expresses this in his Hecuba soliloquy when he tries to understand an actor's display of grief for someone who died thousands of years ago: 'What's Hecuba to him, or he to Hecuba, that he should weep for her?' (*Hamlet* 2.2). Similar to elsewhere in the play, Hamlet – as a representative of the modern human being – contemplates the disjunction between reality and appearance. Today, such profuse and dramatic show of emotion – like the wailing of the professional mourners – is no longer convincing in its authenticity, but originally, such feelings were always genuine. 'The immense lamentation of the gods ... the cosmic lament': that is the key. Apparently, those cults performing the ritual lamentations of the heroes and gods were still able to relive the ancient Lemurian experience. Their experience of minor and major (for there was also great rejoicing when the cultic god was resurrected) were both originally beyond the octave – originally on the macro-level.

Practising a deep gaze towards the dying and resurrecting Christ will allow such macro-soul feelings to develop gradually again in a new way. Modern human beings, who have become emotionally short of breath, need to get to know such deep feelings on a large scale again. These feelings are like the majestic and slow rolling waves of the Atlantic Ocean, rather than our daily ups and downs of pleasure and pain that are like the agitated ripples of a pond. This expansive feeling is healing for the soul, particularly if we are able, for example, even in the deepest personal grief during the Easter period, to reserve a part of our inner life for the jubilation of the resurrection, which we hear of in the Consecration of the Human Being during those forty days.

Rilke gave expression to a sense of the greater dimensions of pain in the last (No. 10) of his *Duino Elegies,* in which he writes about people being caught up in the everyday world of their 'City of Sorrow'. The receptive ones can be led out of this cramped world by the Laments, which appear as elemental genii, into the 'spacious landscape', where 'the mountains of Primal Pain' tower in the distance. 'We were once ... a great family, we Lamentations.'[4]

If we return from such thoughts to our Passion and Easter epistle texts, we can sense that we only do them justice by recognising in them the minor and major beyond the octave.

'O human soul' expresses, as Steiner put it in his lecture, 'the immense lamentation of the gods' for the one who has fallen away from them. As a response to this, we then hear in the Passiontide inserted prayer, 'My self lies lamenting on the ground'. In this response there is some dimension of the cosmic lament of the gods. It does not say 'I lie lamenting', but is instead objectified: 'my self lies lamenting ...' This conveys a cosmic fact, not just a personal complaint. This is the only place where the word 'lamenting' appears in our sacrament. Such a *hapax legomenon*, a word used only once, calls us to bring the right intention when it is spoken in the sacrament.

The inserted prayer continues, 'Raise it, O Spirit ...' In ancient Egypt there was a special ceremony in Memphis to raise again the *djed,* the sacred pillar, which was lying down. This pillar represented Osiris' spine, and its erection celebrated his resurrection.

At Easter, this raising is seen in the resurrection of Christ. 'Christ is risen to you as the meaning of the earth.' In the epistle, the raising, or uplifting, is brought in direct connection to the motif of the word. 'Your word go forth'. Speaking is added to uprightness. The third element contained in 'the meaning of the earth' is thinking, which makes us capable of asking about and grasping meaning.

It is worth looking at the threefold mention of the I (as a noun in its own right, the self) throughout the Passiontide and Easter epistle texts as one movement. This I or self appears three times during the whole season (Passiontide to Easter), and only during Passiontide is it called *my* self; at Easter, the 'my' is withdrawn from the I and we begin hearing about *the* self: 'What heals the self in the ground of the soul', and then, 'Shining is the self.' The disappearance of the possessive ('my') can be compared in a certain way with the metamorphosis in the funeral text, where we move from '*our* dear (name)' to '*the* dear (name)'; in so doing, we reverently release the deceased, withdrawing our personal claim on them, to allow their star to emerge from the clouds.

Instead, the possessive 'my' appears in other contexts at Easter. In the additional prayer at the initial epistle, for instance, we hear about 'my heart ... my spirit ... my breath ... my blood.' It is worth taking note of the unusual nature of these expressions in this context, namely that the 'my' has been taken away from the I and instead, added to 'spirit'. Within the self-contained, small cosmos of words in the Passiontide–Easter texts, this is a noteworthy event: the spirit, perceived as 'lost', has now become 'my spirit'. The initially impersonal-objective spirit becomes personal-objective by individualising itself in the human being. Spirit light through soul warmth.

In the *Philosophy of Freedom* we can find this passage about reaching spirit light through soul warmth, wherein Steiner describes the way ideas can take on unique colouring inside individuals: 'There are people for whom even the most universal ideas entering their heads still retain a special colouring that shows them unmistakably connected with their bearer.'[5]

In the Easter context 'my spirit' is already something like a spirit-self that we sense in advance. It is the one that can feel 'the Vanquisher of Death'. A premonition of this manas (or spirit-self) can perhaps be found in the fervent piety of an Orthodox Easter midnight mass. Likewise, at the end of the hymn-like inserted prayer before the Offertory, we hear of the 'human spirit light'. There are no mere filler words here – everything is precise and concrete.

If, through the celebration of Passion Week and Easter Week our congregations experience a connection to the great minor and major beyond the octave, then we are practising what we can read in *Esoteric Science* about religious life: 'religious feelings leave a uniform imprint on all our thinking, feeling, and willing ... Religious belief, therefore, has a far-reaching effect on our soul.'[6]

Ascension (1963)

Forty years ago, in 1923, the priesthood received the epistles for Ascension and Pentecost in the priests' circular of May 4. Ascension Day fell on May 10, Pentecost on May 20. It is worth noting that directly after sending out those epistles, Rudolf Steiner gave a lecture on May 7: 'The Ascension Revelation and the Mystery of Pentecost'.[7] It would appear that his work for our movement involving the mysteries of the festival cycle led him to deal with Ascension in a special way. As far as I know – please correct me if I'm mistaken – he had never given a lecture with

Ascension as the main theme before this. He first spoke explicitly about Christmas to the members in 1903, and in 1904 also about Easter and Pentecost, but he spoke specifically about Ascension only in 1923.

Certainly, he had mentioned Ascension earlier, alluding to it as an ascent to a higher sphere. Ascension marks the event of Christ ascending to a world even higher than the one he had been inhabiting.[8] For the initiate, ascension to the seventh level (of the Father) is a supreme and ineffable experience. A completely new tone enters with the presentation of the *Fifth Gospel:* 'Instead of entering the realm of the spirit, as human beings do after death, the Christ spirit brought a sacrifice by making its heaven on the earth, as it were.'[9] In a similar lecture later in that year in Hamburg, we find the following: 'God's entry into his earthly existence appeared to the apostles as the Ascension image, thus actually his journey into earth rather than his journey to heaven.'[10]

Ascension is actually his journey into the earth. Steiner said this in 1913 as if mentioning it in passing, when in reality, it is a fundamental correction of a centuries-old misunderstanding. This seedlike announcement in 1913 was then elaborated upon in 1923. The succinct formula – *Ascendit ad coelos* (ascended to the heavens) – combined with the mythical image of the Christ rising was sufficient for the first centuries, when people still had a relationship with the imaginative realm. The dawning of the age of the consciousness soul, however, went hand in hand with the crisis of religious imagination, which has led to today's demythologisation debate.

In 1525, the intellectually radical early Protestants discussed the Lord's Supper with the conservative Martin Luther. Their main argument against the real presence of body and blood was that since the Ascension, these substances were, after all, located in heaven and therefore could not be on the altar.[11] In other words, they held a completely spatial conception of heaven. To make the concept of heaven compatible with the potential omnipresence of body and blood on the altars, Luther made considerable attempts to convey it as supra-spatial, but his argumentation did not convince the others. Only through the new recognition of 'higher worlds' can we regain the concept of heaven, the supreme importance of which can be understood by taking a look at the Lord's Prayer. Rudolf Steiner first restored the concept of heaven to modern consciousness and then later corrected the concept of Ascension.

In Steiner's translation of the Nicene Creed, he left the image in its traditional form: 'And he ascended into heaven and is seated at the right hand of the Father.' On October 8, 1921, he gave us the new Creed, which contains the 'correction' for the first time in Christian liturgical history.[12] The Ascension does not take Christ away from the earth. Rather, it is precisely the prerequisite for his omnipresence and potential omnipotence. This eighth Creed sentence allows the old mythical and powerful but misleading image of the Ascension to fall away. What takes place in this new Creed is a 'demythologisation' that is appropriate for today's world and expresses the essential truth in conceptual language. The old image does find a quiet echo in the term 'heavenly forces', but linking the word 'heavenly' with the word 'forces' moves the term from the pictorial into the conceptual. The correction mainly lies in the words: 'on earth'. The image of 'sitting on the right', is fully translated into the realm of the conceptual.

Steiner's development of the new conceptualisation culminated in May 1923 with the epistle and the lecture of May 7.[13] The lecture resolves the contradiction between the image of the Ascension and the promise spoken by Christ: 'I am with you always' (Mt 28:20). He shows how humanity was in danger of being torn apart. The decay of the physical body threatened its ability to hold on to the etheric body, which for its part was inclined to float against gravity towards the sun. Through the resurrection, a phantom physical body was restored that was able to retain its hold on the etheric body. The Ascension of Christ is indeed an upward motion in that he 'united himself with this striving' (of the etheric body). But on the other hand, He 'holds' it, so to speak – he holds it through the phantom power in the earthly realm of humanity. We can speak of a 'rising', but not a 'departure from the earth'. The Risen (Ascended) One 'holds together' what would otherwise have to fall apart. As Steiner said in that Ascension lecture, 'The mighty scene of the Ascension is that of the *rescue of the physical-etheric nature of man by Christ.*' It is an ascension that can benefit earthly existence precisely through its upward movement, just as Archimedes sought a point outside the earth to be able to lift it out of its position. The image of the ascended Christ thus takes on a completely different quality.

This corrected concept of the Ascension has now found its way into our epistle in the form of sacramental words that express the concept with marvellous power: 'To heavenly being for the sake of earthly being.'

This epistle is particularly close to the Creed in terms of its content. Not only does it echo the Creed's statements regarding salvation, it sketches a summary of Christology even while seeming to deliberately avoid mentioning the name of Christ (we first hear him mentioned in the inserted prayer). It gives the impression that this name should be withdrawn from use and only be filled again with the meaning that truly belongs to it, so as to prevent it from becoming an empty sound.

Again and again in the epistle and inserted prayer we hear of 'earthly being'. As with the word 'heavenly powers' in the Creed, the concrete word 'earth' is here connected with a conceptual component, namely, 'being'. The word 'heaven' only appears after we hear the idea of 'transfiguring earthly being', through which we progress directly to the phrase 'heavenly being'. Only now does the epistle approach the old imagination – in this respect going further than the more intellectual Creed – but now, arriving at this imagination anew: 'His elevation to heavenly being.' In the inserted prayer we then encounter the image of the clouds, but here, too, with the conceptual element added to it: 'the being of the clouds'. The old misunderstanding is averted by the preceding sign of 'beholding', whereby the whole event is transposed from the spatial-local into the supersensible.

Just as in the Creed, the old image of 'sitting on the right' is entirely transposed into the realm of thinking. One recognises its meaning in the phrase, 'in that he dwells with you,' in the motif of the transfiguration of the earthly, and in the fulfilment of the Act of Consecration through the 'power' of the one who has gone to the Father. Only as such does the Christ have authority over all flesh.

Like the Creed, the epistle also commemorates Christ's Ascension in the present tense: in both the Creed and the epistle we hear 'He lives ...' A new situation was established through the Ascension event – a situation that continues to the present day, out of which we must learn to behold the etheric Christ in the clouds of heaven.

In addition to having a clear connection to the Creed, the epistle also has a special relationship to the Transubstantiation. John 6:62 foreshadows the Ascension as the cognitive key to the reality of the Eucharist, for it is only through the Ascension that the body and blood attain the status by which they can be present on altars in an elevated state and can then be offered as Communion. It was the loss of the understanding of the Ascension that led to the loss of the reality of Communion.

Like the Transubstantiation, the epistle also takes the form of a direct prayer to God the Father, particularly the words at the beginning of the epistle. These words were also prayed to the Father God in the old Mass, after the recitation of the Gospel. The epistle addresses the Father three times directly. 'You who wield ...' refers to the ground of existence. 'You have sent him' implies that the Father let the Son go forth from himself. 'He dwells with you' refers to the community of divine persons in the Holy Spirit.

The actual process of Transubstantiation reaches something like a consummation in the lifting up of the bread and cup, accompanied by the words, 'let the bread be ...' and 'let the wine be ...'. It is worth noting how often the word 'be' is used in this epistle, whereas 'becoming' plays a corresponding role during Advent. Thus we move from becoming to being. Being is particularly associated with the Father. The result of the Transubstantiation is fixed, as it were, in being: the bread 'is' Christ's body. Is it merely a coincidence then, that the very words 'let ... be' are linked with the raising of the substances, that is with the symbolism of the Ascension?

The Offertory also contains a raising of the cup; however, it differs in that in the Offertory it is primarily a question of breaking the spell of gravity, the consequence of the Fall, and to allow the upward striving motion to regain its strength. For all intents and purposes, it is the counter-movement to the Fall, which we hear in the accompanying words, where the emphasis is on the upward gesture: 'So that ... can also raise itself to the heavens.'

Just as we hear of heaven and earth during the Offertory, as well as of upward and downward, we hear the same at the end of the Transubstantiation at the lifting of the cup. At that point, however, it is expressed differently. Referring to the words that directly precede the 'let ... be', the focus is not just on the 'upward', but on the effect of grace coming from above downwards: the substances are raised to the One who works from above, lifted out of their material weight to be able to fully absorb the power of grace working earthwards, and to radiate; the monstrance (the vessel used in the Catholic mass) is an image of this radiating.

This lifting up is an ascension, but not in the sense of 'away from the earth'. It seeks that level above the earth where the Risen One works 'for the sake of earthly being' – that point where downward-working and upward-striving forces interweave harmoniously. We see the same image in the Christ who has ascended to cloud-existence, as he turns back towards the earth to bestow a blessing. The Christ reveals himself in heights that are not turned away from the earth, but are open in such a way that they can absorb what is of earth into themselves. In this way, the raising of the substances during the Transubstantiation has an Ascension quality.

Almost every time the word 'heaven' appears in our rituals, it does so in conjunction with the word 'earth'.

Emil Bock always felt that we should do more to celebrate the festival of the Ascension. Despite the passing of 40 years, we are still faced with the task of creating a place for the renewed meaning of this important festival in our congregations' consciousness and feeling life.

St John's Tide (1963)

The St John's Tide epistle is the last that Rudolf Steiner gave us. Koschützki, Meyer and Wistinghausen received it in June 1924 during the agricultural course in Koberwitz.[14] This background of rescuing the life of the earth by tapping into the cosmic forces is certainly significant with respect to our celebration of St John's.

The written form of the epistle is noticeably divided into seven sections. With the exception of the Trinity epistle (three paragraphs), this is not the case with any other epistle. This division of the epistle text shows a loosening up reminiscent of a dispersal of clouds that allows the blue sky to shine through. In *The Cycle of the Year,* the lecture cycle on the seasons given at Easter 1923, there is a drawing by Rudolf Steiner showing how the breath of the earth begins to push outwards at Easter time, meeting with the growing power of the sun that is flooding inwards towards the earth. A corresponding drawing illustrates the St John's Tide period, where that breath is completely outside and it is not the sun but the stars that appear at its boundary. Our St John's epistle is like an image of this exhalation of life upwards to the starry realms. It is perhaps therefore justifiable to look at – and feel into – its seven paragraphs through this lens.

With all due reserve I would say that it has always made sense to me to connect these seven sections with the seven planetary qualities of cosmic evolution. The first part is linked to Saturn, and then it continues through in the order of the planetary evolutionary phases. The second verse, culminating in 'the Christ-Sun', is quite sunlike. In the third verse, the entry into the 'guilt-laden ... field of earth' is reminiscent of the moon. In the fourth verse, which is exactly the centre of the whole text, we hear of John the Baptist and his 'guilt-conscious word of flame', which we can see as an image of Mars. Mars and Mercury represent the two halves of the earth's development: the first half, which brings the descent into guilt, takes place during the Mars stage; the second, with the beginning of redemptive work, happens during the stage of healing Mercury. Thus, the fifth verse is about the act of salvation (life born out of death) with the resulting new impetus towards 'the pure ether-spheres'. The sixth stanza shines brightly in the wisdom-light of Jupiter (knowing, revealing), without a shadow of guilt. Finally, the seventh stanza is, as Hermann Beckh called it, a manifestation of Venus Urania; it is the sacred marriage of the soul with the Bridegroom of Light ('light's fullness of love').[15]

The visible sun disc will disappear in the middle of the Venus stage, as will all visible cosmic appearance. According to Steiner:

> This fiery sphere of the sun will not continue its existence beyond the Venus age; it will then disappear … What will remain beyond Venus existence has its germinal essence only in man. Christ had to come to man from the cosmic expanses if he wished to embark with man on the path to eternity.[16]

This implies that during the Venus stage, the sun-nature of Christ will have fully entered the soul and spirit of man.

Hans Feddersen pointed out how certain echoes of our ritual texts can be found in Goethe's works.[17] We can think of Goethe's 'Blessed Yearning', a mystery-poem he composed in Wiesbaden in the week of St John's Tide, on July 31, 1814:

> No more in darkness canst thou rest,
> Waited upon by shadows blind,
> A new desire has thee possessed
> For procreant joys of loftier kind.[18]

The death by flame that Goethe portrays in this poem is a true Johannine fire, and the culminating call to 'die and become!' in the poem corresponds to the deed of life and death on Golgotha.

It has often been noted that St John's Tide is the only festival period in which a direct invocation is made, which is not to the Trinitarian persons themselves. Johannes Perthel once pointed out that Moses is mentioned in the breviary, while John-Elijah is mentioned in the Act of Consecration.[19] The soul of the old Adam who fell into sin lived alongside the angelic being within John the Baptist – hence the motif of 'guilt', which is fourfold: 'the guilt-laden seed of humanity'; the 'guilt-conscious word of flame' in John the Baptist; for us 'guilty human beings', and the prospect of being raised again to 'the guiltless ... on the glancing waves of Spirit'. The invocation of Elijah-John takes place after the last words of the Offertory, in order to summon the Elijah-John fire through prayer before entering into the Transubstantiation.

However, the 'New Adam' is also invoked in these texts in a direct form as never before in the epistles. We experienced earlier how the contemplative style of the epistles turns at particular points into the direct 'you' of prayer – to the 'divine world power,' to the 'Fatherly Ground of the World'. Here at St John's Tide, Christ himself is invoked with a unique directness in the words 'Christ-Sun', and subsequently 'You, our Deliverer, entered ... humanity, needy of healing.'

The word 'Christ-Sun' is quite probably the centre of the whole epistle. Rudolf Meyer, writing for our priests' circular years ago – how I wish that he could have continued his epistle reflections that were so helpful and inspiring for us back then! – highlighted the following three lines of the epistle:

> *They work in the flowing ether-light*
> *They create in the living world of being*
> *They ripen in the midst of the world.*

He pointed out that they can be connected with what Steiner described in the London lecture on the threefold sun.[20] The ancient Persians experienced the essence of the Sun-Spirit, the Egyptians and Babylonians experienced its astral powers, and the Greeks felt its etheric effects in the atmosphere.

He also spoke about the threefold sun in the lecture on August 24, 1918 (sun-body, sun-soul, 'Helios'; sun-spirit, 'the primal good'), and on November 6, 1921, soon after our Autumn Course, where he portrayed the sun as the divine source of light for Zarathustra, the divine source of life for the third civilisation, and the divine source of love for the Greeks.[21]

This is then echoed in the three aforementioned lines of the epistle. The word love itself does not appear in the last line, but is essentially encapsulated in the 'Christ-Sun' and is then finally also pronounced directly at the end of the epistle.

In his discussion of the threefold sun on both November 6, 1921 and on April 24, 1922, Rudolf Steiner mentioned Emperor Julian and his *Hymn to King Helios*. The way that this aspect of Christianity expands itself into the cosmos in our epistle serves to 'bring Julian home' to Christianity. In fact, one point in our text seems to echo Julian directly, namely where the Deliverer enters into humanity 'in the Sun-Spirit's ether rays'. In Julian's ode to the sun we find the following:

> For from him [Helios] are we born, and by him are we nourished. But his more divine gifts, and all that he bestows on our souls when he frees them from the body and then lifts them up on high to the region of those substances that are akin to the god; and the fineness and vigour [*Eu-tonon*] of his divine rays, which are assigned as a sort of vehicle [*ochema*] for the safe descent of our souls into this world of generation; all this, I say, let others celebrate in fitting strains, but let me believe it rather than demonstrate its truth.[22]

Here, he is hinting at the secrets of the sunrays, namely that they are the vehicle for the soul descending into an earthly birth. They are husked (*lepton* literally translates to husk or sheath) and *eu-tonon,* taut in a good way. *Tonus* (or tenor) means tension in Latin. We find this root in the word for muscle tension, atony, and the tension of the reverberating string that creates a *tone*. The Stoics contrasted the material element in the creation of the world with the 'tenor' as a supersensible factor.[23]

Six months before distributing the St John's epistle, on January 11, 1924, Rudolf Steiner spoke about the sun-birth originally intended for human beings:

> We are in reality, according to the view that prevailed in those olden times, beings of the sun. In our whole nature and existence we are united with the sun. And we ought, as humans, as solar beings, to have had an altogether different relationship to the earth. What should have happened is that the earth, first of all, should obey her impulse to bring forth out of the mineral and plant kingdoms the human seed in etheric form, and the sun should then fructify the seed. Then should arise the etheric human form which, by establishing its own relationship to the physical substances of the earth, should then take on earthly substantiality ... The seeds of humanity should grow up out of the earth with the purity of vegetable life, appearing here and there as ethereal fruits, darkly gleaming. These should then in a certain season of the year be overshone by the light of the sun.[24]

Instead of this happening, there was the fall into heredity. The Gothic Bishop Ulfilas coined the term 'human seed'. When the Christ descended to earth, this happened 'in the Sun-spirit's ether rays'.

The language of our rituals avoids the specific terms of anthroposophy (with a few exceptions, such as 'spirit land' or 'formative forces'), however, at St John's Tide the word 'ether' is used four times. When answering questions on July 12, 1923, Rudolf Steiner also said that under certain circumstances, one could simply speak of the etheric body in front of a congregation.[25] This would probably not be possible if the last centuries had not done the groundwork. Just as Fichte defined the 'ego', the literature of the eighteenth century brought a spiritual connotation to the word 'etheric' or 'ethereal'. The word was transferred from the technical books of the alchemists into the cosmopolitan language of the educated. While another branch of its meaning developed downwards, so to speak, into materiality, the great poets helped the word 'ether' maintain its quality of being a window to the supersensible.

In *Dichtung und Wahrheit* [*From my Life: Poetry and Truth*], Goethe speaks of the 'marvellous' Alsace: 'For months, pure ethereal mornings delighted us, where the sky showed itself in all its splendour by soaking the earth with an abundance of dew.' (Part 3, Book 11). From this description of Alsace one gets a sense of the etheric. In *Faust* one hears about the 'ethereal twilight' and 'ether in the clear', just to name a few examples. In his novel *Wilhelm Meister's Journeyman Years* he wrote about the 'shining space of the ether' visible while gazing at the stars (Book 1, Ch. 10), and in the same book, we find the 'ethereal' Makaria poem (Ch. 15). Turning to Novalis, we find 'The miraculous home evaporated into the ether', or 'My blood transformed into balm and ether'. Hölderlin, in particular, repeatedly glorified the 'ether' like no other.[26] This is how this word was rescued through the period of materialism and could now be incorporated into the Christian sacraments.

A unique phrase is the 'the midst of the world', that is directly connected to the 'Christ-Sun'. This gesture at midsummer portrays a kind of counter-effect to the natural seasonal gesture (concentration in winter, dissolution in summer). In a similar way, our Advent service – near midwinter – speaks of 'the bounds of the all'. (That same 'all' is significantly found in the Sunday children's service.) At Easter we hear of 'the air around the earth', whereas at St John's Tide we hear, 'in the sphere around his body'. We see how the Sun-Christ appears in conjunction with the centre. In the Gospel of John, the Christ is connected with the mystery of the centre both at the beginning and at the end. 'In your midst [*mesos hymōn*] stands one you do not know' (Jn 1:26). The following could also resonate with this: in the centre of your being he stands still veiled, not yet recognised as the true self. After the resurrection it is stated twice explicitly that 'Jesus came and stood among them', that is, in the midst, at their centre (Jn 20:19, 26).

To return once again to Goethe, during the first visit to Makaria, Wilhelm Meister contemplates the 'splendour of the ether', and says:

> 'What am I in the face of universe?' he asked his spirit.
> 'How can I stand before it, stand in its very midst?' ...
> 'How can man confront the infinite except by gathering all his spiritual forces, which are drawn in all directions, into the innermost, deepest part of his being, by asking himself: "Have you the right even to imagine yourself in the midst of this eternally living order if there does not immediately manifest itself inside you something in continuous motion, revolving around a pure centre? And even if it would be difficult for you to find this centre in your own breast, you would recognise it because a benevolent, beneficent effect emanates from it and testifies to its existence".'[27]

Michaelmas (1963)

The relationship between humanity and history is currently going through a crisis. A wave of historical confusion is spreading, along with a reaction against the historicism of the nineteenth century.[28]

In the meantime, anthroposophy has brought us a new conceptualisation of history. The role history plays is one of the main differences between anthroposophy and Indian-influenced theosophy. The amount of space the topic of history occupies in Rudolf Steiner's lectures must have something to do with anthroposophy's Michaelic background. As an echo of ancient wisdom, theosophy is not tied to the historiography of the Gabriel age, which more or less records the 'deeds of the fathers'. It is Michael's influence that reveals how deeply the I and 'history' belong together.

Rather than seeing history as a conglomeration of events that happen to people who are basically thought of as 'finished' in their evolution, we should think of history as the process whereby the true essence of the human being gradually manifests itself. Individuals awakening to the I need a knowledge that makes them aware of their own place to stand and act from within the great stream of human becoming. It took a long time for humanity to consciously permeate space and grasp the time-space orientation. We are now increasingly faced with the necessity of finding our way in the historical element of time.

Earlier historical observation was a kind of substitute for the lost hereditary memory of the experiences of the ancestors. It gravitated towards the primordial beginnings, and often began, if not with the creation of the world, with Adam and Eve. While our present situation could at best be felt in its alarming remoteness from the beginnings and golden prehistoric times, the way we saw history did not give us any experience of future-oriented meaning as a point of passage on our apocalyptic path.

Michael, who has a special relationship with history due to his relationship with Christ, inspired the important preparatory period from the sixth century BC until late in the Alexander period. He experienced Christ's departure from the sun, and, as the seventh and last of his fellow archangels, began his first post-Christian reign only in 1879. Although he was the 'last' of the seven, Michael was the first among them to strive to harmonise his work completely with the changed situation since Golgotha. He heralds the first reign of the sun after the turning point in time. Unlike the foregoing ages, this reign no longer carries elements of the pre-Christian world. He brings the 'sun-consequence' of Christianity, so to speak, and radically changes its mode of action, its 'method'. More than for the other archangels, the difference between pre-Christian and post-Christian times is a profound experience for Michael.

This makes him the great 'teacher of history' for our time, which shines through in our Michaelmas epistle. First of all, it contains the necessary basic historical orientation. The difference between 'once upon a time' and 'these days' is convincingly demonstrated for the modern Christian: 'once', Michael had to adapt his work to the Father principle, whereas 'in these world days' he metamorphoses it in harmony with the Son principle, which was made fully manifest through Golgotha. This view of history is decisively characterised by its recognition of the differences between the pre- and post-Christian eras.

But this is not the end of the story. The illumination of our position today goes into even more detail, and a second juxtaposition emerges: 'in years past' and 'today'. It moves thus closer to us in time, giving us a glimpse of that moment when the sun-element in Christianity will emerge in a potent way.

The conspicuous collection of time-oriented words in the Michaelmas epistle has already been mentioned many times in our circle. *Hour, day* and *year* are found there together. Likewise, *moment, today, now.* The *once* is joined by the temporal *before in years past* follows *before* the gentleness of Christ. In this way, it is truly an epistle of the spirit of the times. Following the word 'today' comes the word that Michael himself speaks in a personal address directly to the individual. It tells how Christ's death and resurrection continues to have an effect ('the deed of life and death' is an alternative term used also at other points in Christian Community sacraments to denote the Mystery of Golgotha): the phrase 'working on' implies that this deed accomplished on earth continues dynamically in the supersensible (impetus for an eternal movement), whereby what happened in the past becomes the living present. At the same time, apocalyptic horizons emerge, as we hear in the last words of both the epistle and the inserted prayer: 'through all cycles of time'.

It is part of the specifically Michaelic aspect that this continued working be understood as being dependent on us human beings, or as the epistle puts it, 'the earthly human being'. Christ becomes the saviour of the earthly human being through his deed carried out in the realm of earthly humanity. His deed can also only truly be born within the earthly human being, for we alone, not the angels, are born to understand, honour and continue the events of Golgotha. (Which is not a contradiction to the fact that in times of human darkness, the angels are the ones who safeguard the insights relating to Golgotha). The sacrifice of Christ can only achieve its full continuing effect if it is able to come to life 'in' and 'through the earthly human being. On the way, the Golgotha power will be able to appear in the future through human beings in a world-creating way – as the epistle states, 'creating into times to come'. The order of the words 'deed', 'working on' and 'creating' in the epistle is thus quite significant.

Finally, the Michaelmas epistle also contains the great modern myth of cosmic intelligence and its destinies. This modern myth, if I may put it that way, was only really presented in 1924 in Rudolf Steiner's lectures in Arnhem (July 19) and Dornach (July 28) and in the last lecture of our Apocalypse Course.[29] He wrote the classic presentation from his sickbed in the autumn of that year.[30] The essence of this myth, however, is already contained in our epistle, which we received in the first half of September 1923, in the form that is relevant to our sacrament.

In the final words of the epistle, the 'heavenly light' is in danger of being extinguished in the 'earthly light' – not in the earthly *darkness,* but in the earthly *light.* In this context, this ambiguous expression (it could also be understood in a Christmas sense) takes on an eerie nuance. It is the intelligence, which is threatened by the Ahrimanic and has sunk down to earth, that wants to emancipate itself from the primordial light, in the same way that bright street lighting at night blocks out the stars. The phrase 'earthly light' is much more eerie here than the word 'darkness' would be, although ultimately, this blindingly bright dead light represents the most dangerous manifestation of satanic darkness. The concern for the threatened heavenly light is placed on the shoulders of human beings, whom Michael determines to be ready to bear this concern together with the gods.

The salvation of the 'heavenly light' is only possible through the continuing effect of Golgotha in earthly human beings. Only then will humanity not only have a past, but also a real future. There is a doxology from the original Latin mass: *sicut erat in principio, et nunc, et semper, et in saecula saeculorum.* This is most commonly translated as 'Glory to the Father, and to the Son, and to the Holy Spirit. As it was in the beginning, is now, and ever shall be, world without end.' This threefold formula spans the past, present and future. Such a complete reference to time is reserved in our worship for special use in the Michaelmas season. The prospect of 'through all cycles of time' is often found, especially in the Communion, which is a foretaste of a distant fulfilment. At Easter, the 'now' of the present is added. Realising that the full Trinity of past-present-future only appears at Michaelmas highlights its omission in the rest of the sacramental texts. The words 'from the beginning' resound with Michael's faithfulness to the primordial light.

The 'is to shine' also has its own special flavour. It is not a 'must'; nor is it a 'should'. Rather, within the is-to-be-so lies the potential for freedom. We see before us the original intention of the gods, as it was meant to be from the beginning, and we are free to place ourselves at the disposal of this intention. The word 'free' is also present in the epistle ('the free power'). No commandment is given, but the human disposition towards the possibility of freedom is highlighted.

The Michaelmas epistle contains the special mysteries of our time in concentrated form. It provides an answer to what Goethe admonishes in the Makaria chapter of *Wilhelm Meister's Journeyman Years:* 'Ask yourself, how do you relate to day and hour?'[31]

The altar in the epistles (1963)

Not counting the seasonally neutral Trinity epistle and the epistle given for the inauguration of erzoberlenker, the number of actual epistles for the course of the year is twelve. They were apparently written individually, from one festival season to the next, between Christmas 1922 and St John's Tide 1924. In the end there were twelve of them; they all flowed from a single inspirational background, and together form one body.

The expression just used – that they were created 'individually' from season to season – is not entirely accurate. The twelve epistles did not come to us from our teacher in twelve individual messages, but in seven. They were apparently brought forth from the spiritual world in seven different inspirational experiences. The first three transmissions are each groups of epistles, which in themselves form independent smaller organisms within the great twelve.

Christmas 1922 marks the beginning of the seasonal epistles, with the 'original mass' at midnight being the very first seasonal epistle given to us. Together with it came the texts for the other two Christmas services. The three epistles – this is clear to us all – are organically connected: they lead from the rapture of 'the land of spirits' (here an anthroposophic term is introduced into the language of Christian worship) to the indwelling of the earthly body, and they are held together by the words spoken facing the congregation: 'Know this ...'

These three Christmas epistles and the insertion of the names of the hierarchies are, incidentally, the only annual texts of the Consecration of the Human Being that have a parallel in the old mass. Anyone who reads the Oratio and the Preface (before the beginning of the consecration) placed between the Gloria and the reading of the epistles in the Christmas masses will recognise the parallels and also the differences that stand out. When we met in Dornach in 1921, Rudolf Steiner compared our new service to the text of the old mass. He could have done the same with the Christmas mass – but not after that, for the later festival epistles are absolutely new territory, in the sense of the return of Christ in the etheric and the completely new elements associated with that. But at its root, our new touches the old 'original mass' in the Christmas experience, in the sense of the 'continuity' in the progress of spiritual life that Rudolf Steiner always spoke of.

This continuity is also related to the fact that he read the beginning of the Christmas Mass to us in Latin during the first sermon to priests. He read it from Nils Gihr's *Das Heilige Messopfer,* which was found in his estate, with occasional underlining and bracketing. Unfortunately, no one can remember exactly what he read at the time. It could have been the beginning of the Christmas mass, the Oratio of the Midnight Mass, or it could have been the Preface, which is explicitly marked up with pencil.

With the next wave of epistle inspiration, which reached us at the beginning of February 1923, the parallels to the old text of the mass cease completely apart from very slight echoes in the Easter insertion of the Exultet of the Holy Saturday liturgy (*gaudeat et tellus ... orbis*). Here we have another trinity – Passion, Holy Week, and Easter – forming a whole, as if from a single mould. The metamorphosis of the blood-breath mystery runs through these three epistle texts, making them appear closely related.

The last group is formed by Ascension and Pentecost, the epistles for which we received at the beginning of May 1923. Both epistles have the same number of lines. A gospel pericope taken from the farewell discourses is added to each. The 'relationship' is otherwise less close than in the previous groups, but they are still siblings, so to speak.

The fourth gift of this kind, which we received on its own in September 1923, was the Michaelmas epistle. We then received the Advent epistle in October 1923. At the beginning of January 1924 (just in time for January 6) the Epiphany epistle, and finally, in June 1924 in Koberwitz, the St John's Tide texts.

These seven waves of inspiration for the course of the year each have their own character and style, but together they form a whole.

A trace of this organic coherence can be seen in the fact that the word 'altar' appears in each of the four seasonal archangel quarters, nuanced differently each time in a significant way. Our year begins with Advent: 'deeply musing as we stand before the altar'.

The altar as resurrection tomb *and* table is the basic symbol of Christian worship, or in a broader sense, of worship in general. As far as I know, the altar first appears as a significant symbol in Rudolf Steiner's work in 1904 in his book, *How to Know Higher Worlds,* in the chapter 'Life and Death, the Great Guardian of the Threshold'. If we decide to follow the demands of the figure of light, we 'offer up our gifts and talents on the sacrificial altar of humanity'.[32]

In the same year, he uses the image of the altar in *Theosophy.* In the chapter on the aura, he writes of those who prove themselves to be 'servants of the eternal' as the 'flames used by the divinity to enlighten this world ... they show ... the extent to which they have wrested from their narrower selves the capacity to offer themselves up on the great altar of cosmic activity.'[33] This passage may stand out as being quite special the very first time you read it. The otherwise deliberately sober tone of the book takes on a religious solemnity here. For a moment, a curtain is torn, a veil is lifted. The book *Theosophy* holds the Christ mystery like a secret sealed within this seemingly apocalyptic image of this 'great altar of cosmic activity'.

Seven years later, when Rudolf Steiner gave an inside perspective on world evolution in the intimate cycle *Inner Experiences of Evolution,* he spoke of 'the altar of the cosmic all' in connection with the sacrifice of the Thrones.[34] In the karma lecture of June 27, 1924 – after the founding of The Christian Community – he spoke about the derivation of the altar design out of that vision: 'Such was the origin of the altar'.[35]

The very first sentence of the Advent epistle contains the word 'altar'. 'As we stand before the altar' may remind us of a phrase from Steiner's autobiography about having stood spiritually before the Mystery of Golgotha.[36] In the Advent activity of our souls becoming 'deeply musing' lies the seed of what can one day become the innermost, most serious celebration of knowledge.

'Before the altar …' As a new beginning, the Advent season should teach us, deep down in our feeling life, that Christianity is still 'ahead of us'. This finds its spatial and pictorial expression in the deep musing in front of the altar, which we gaze at from the outside.

The altar appears a second time at Easter, in the inserted prayer that leads us from the Gospel Reading into the Offertory. Easter – precisely the region of the mystery of death and life – is when we find a connection with the tomb. (The aspect of the table is found in the Priest Ordination). The I that has been dark lights up: the grave of the soul becomes an altar. It is the Christ himself, who now enters and performs his great sacrifice at this altar of the soul. This 'microcosmic' stage in the soul of an earthly human being loses nothing of its cosmic dimensions; it goes out 'to the worlds afar, to the earth near'. If the Christ himself steps up to the altar of the soul as the sacrificer, then the Offertory becomes a true reality.

The third mention of the altar is found in the St John's Tide inserted prayer, which this time has its place in the even more intimate interval between the Offertory and the Transubstantiation. John is called upon to 'look upon the deed of the altar'. This deed, which we now want to worthily fulfil, is the Transubstantiation. Through Christ's blessing, man himself may become a co-performer of the act of redemption. Here, the altar is the scene of the transformation.

And finally in the very first sentence of the epistle at Michaelmas, again as in Advent, the mention of the altar. 'In this hour from the altar we are to experience in our heart'. As at Advent (that is, in the first and in the last seasonal epistle), the solemn name of the Act of Consecration is spoken.

'From the altar' – this 'from' in the first line of the Michaelmas epistle irritated some of us at the time. Was it a mistake? Was it rather supposed to be – like in the Advent epistle – 'before the altar'? [The difference in German comes down to one letter: *von* or *vor*.]

We are meant to 'experience it in our hearts'. The other day I received a letter in French writing of '*un erlebnis*', using the German word [rather than the French *expérience*]. *Erlebnis* is indeed difficult to translate. At the time of the youth movement, this word became a more dreamlike expression for deep longings that did not quite reach the light of consciousness. It was used a lot and has suffered somewhat as a result. Nevertheless – it has entered the modern ritual language, just as 'the I' and 'consciousness' from philosophy, and 'the ground of the soul' from medieval mysticism. [The German *erleben* (to experience) is related to *Leben* (life)] 'Life' is a word that is particularly characteristic of the Communion in our sacrament, where it is heard repeatedly. Experiencing is the conscious, I-driven appropriation of life.

At the beginning of the Christian year, we have the altar 'before us' and begin to muse deeply in view of this symbol. At the corresponding end of the year, at Michaelmas, the Consecration of the Human Being that has taken place throughout the year is summarised as if in a crowning act of Communion: an innermost appropriation, 'experienced in the heart'.

The 'from' [*von*] is therefore not a spelling mistake. There is a rightness to it. 'From the altar we are to experience' surely implies that what we experience is precisely *from* the altar. At Advent, we stand before what we still have ahead of us. By contrast, at Michaelmas, as if in anticipation of a future final communion, the process moves in the opposite direction: it flows *from* the altar into the heart of the human being and becomes an experience – in the full, life-filled sense of the word.

The altar thus appears four times in the texts of the epistles throughout the course of the year. These four are integrated into the context of the four main parts of the service, into which the fullness of the altar event unfolds.

The Epistles and Inserted Prayers

The versions of the epistles used in North America and in Great Britain and Ireland follow on left and right pages respectively. The translations are from 2024, but may change as they are continually being worked on.

The inserted prayer is spoken after the Creed, except at Christmas and St John's Tide when it is after the Offertory.

Trinity

Conscious of our humanity, we feel the divine Father.
He is in all that we are.
Our substance is his substance.
Our being is his being.
He moves in us through all existence.

Aware of the Christ in our humanity, we feel the divine Son.
He wields through the world as Spirit-Word.
He creates in all that we create.
Our existing is his creating.
Our life is his creating life.
He creates through us in all the soul's creating.

Grasping the Spirit through our humanity, we feel the healing God.
May he shine through the world as Spirit-light.
May he shine in all that we behold.
Our beholding be drenched with his Spirit-light.
May he graciously receive our knowing into his life shining with spirit.
May he fill with spirit all the ways of our human soul.

Advent

Our souls become deeply musing
As we stand before the altar;
The Consecration of the Human Being
Becomes a divining of the spirit;
The veil of the soul spreads
Before the gaze of the spirit eye.
All becomes still before the spirit eye.
There can be heard in the ground of the soul

THE EPISTLES AND INSERTED PRAYERS (AMERICAN / BRITISH)

Trinity

Conscious of our humanity, we feel the divine Father.
He is in all that we are.
Our substance is his substance.
Our being is his being.
He moves in us through all existence.

Aware of the Christ in our humanity, we feel the divine Son.
He wields through the world as Spirit-Word.
He creates in all that we create.
Our existing is his creating.
Our life is his creating life.
He creates through us in all the soul's creating.

Grasping the Spirit through our humanity, we feel the
   healing God.
May he shine through the world as Spirit-light.
May he shine in all that we behold.
Our beholding be drenched with his Spirit-light.
May he graciously receive our knowing into his life
   shining with spirit.
May he fill with spirit all the ways of our human soul.

Advent

Our souls fall deeply musing
As we stand before the altar;
The Act of Consecration of Man
Grows into a divining of the spirit.
The veil of the soul spreads
Before the gaze of the eye of the spirit.
All becomes still before the eye of the spirit.
There can be heard in the ground of the soul

The working of the Father-Ground of the World.
The world calm around us
Fills with the sounding power
That speaks with promise
In the hoping human heart.
Divine Might of Worlds,
You who gleam in the chariot of the sun
You who shine in the bow of colour
Spanning the sky:
You speak in the inner place of the soul.
Yet your speaking
Is no present sounding,
Is future word that softly
Carries into the present.
A 'Become' it speaks
And divining it awakens
The picture of human becoming
In which God's becoming lies hidden.
God's becoming, which in grace
Would shelter and redeem
Our errors, full of mercy
In his own divine soul.
Our heart can sense
The salvation, that in the womb of worlds
Quickens in promise,
That in the inmost soul
Of the mysteries of the world,
Comforting human beings,
Prophetic in dark world night,
Speaks, announcing its work
In the realm of earth.
Working in the realm of earth,
That speaks prophetically
In the gleaming of the chariot of the sun
In the shining of the bow of colour
That spans the sky.

The working of the World's Father Ground.
The world calm around us
Fills with this sounding power
That speaks with promise
Within the hoping heart of man.
Divine Might of Worlds,
You who gleam in the chariot of the sun,
You who shine in the bow of colour
Spanning the skies:
You are speaking in the inner place of the soul.
Yet your speaking
Is no present sounding,
Is future word that quietly
Carries into the present.
'Become' it speaks.
And dawning, it awakens
The picture of man's becoming
In which God's becoming lies hidden.
God's becoming, which in grace
Would mercifully shelter
And redeem our errors
In his own divine soul.
Our heart can sense the salvation
That quickens in promise
In the womb of worlds,
That speaks prophetically
In the inmost soul of the mysteries of the world;
Comforting man,
In dark world night,
Announcing its work
In the realm of earth,
Working in the realm of earth,
It speaks prophetically
In the gleaming of the chariot of the sun,
In the shining of the bow of colour
Spanning the skies.

Inserted prayer

> Twilight holds sway
> In the bounds of the all.
> The gleaming of the chariot of the sun,
> The shining of the bow of colour,
> Spanning the sky:
> They fade into far expanses.
> Divining grows from twilight,
> Sun-chariot shining
> Colour-bow-gleaming
> Beget themselves anew;
> Hail to our divining
> Hail to our hoping,
> Hail to the light-born
> Hail to the colour-carried
> Eternal, divine-wielding
>   Word.

Christmas

Midnight service:

> Into earth-night
> Into sense-darkness
> Streams the Spirit's
> Healing light of grace.
> It streams forth to us
> When we walk
> Freed from the body in the land of spirits
> After the heart within us
> Has felt it in divining prayer.

Inserted prayer

> Twilight holds sway
> In the bounds of the world.
> The gleaming of the chariot of the sun,
> The shining of the bow of colour
> Spanning the skies:
> They fade into far expanses.
> Out of the twilight there dawns divining.
> Sun-chariot-shining
> Colour-bow-gleaming
> Beget themselves anew.
> Hail to our divining,
> Hail to our hoping,
> Hail to the one born of light,
> Hail to the one the colours bear,
> > The eternal,
> > Divine-wielding Word.

Christmas

Midnight service:

> Into earth night
> Into sense darkness
> The light of the Spirit streams
> With healing grace.
> It streams forth to us
> When we walk
> Freed from the body in the land of spirit-beings
> After the heart within us
> Has felt it in divining prayer.

Dawn service:

> Fatherly Ground of the World:
> Our soul feels the drawing near
> Of the healing Creator-Word;
> May his power stream to us in blessing,
> That he touch our speaking lips,
> And warm our speech-bearing blood
> And strengthen our spirit-devoted willing
> Through all future cycles of time.

Morning service:

> Christ, the revealing Creator-Spirit
> Of the Fatherly Ground of the World
> Has chosen the earthly body
> In which he would dwell,
> To save us
> From the deceiving false light,
> To save us
> From the senses' unworthy craving
> In all future cycles of time.

Following the epistle (at all three services)

(From centre of the altar, facing the congregation, also at the end)
       Know this:
The Christ has appeared in the realm of earth
       Behold in him:
The bringer of healing to earthly human beings
Through him has become manifest:
       The Father-Ground of all Being.

THE EPISTLES AND INSERTED PRAYERS (AMERICAN / BRITISH)

Dawn service:

> *Fatherground of the world:*
> *Our soul is aware that the*
> *Creator's healing Word draws near.*
> *May his power stream to us in blessing*
> *That it may touch our speaking lips*
> *And warm our speech-bearing blood*
> *And strengthen our spirit-devoted willing*
> *Through all cycles of time to be.*

Morning service:

> *Christ, the revealing Creator Spirit*
> *Of the Fatherground of the world*
> *Has chosen the earthly body,*
> *Wherein it pleases him to dwell,*
> *To free mankind*
> *From the vain show of illusion,*
> *To free mankind*
> *From the senses' unworthy craving*
> *In all cycles of time to be.*

Following the epistle (at all three services)

(From centre of the altar, facing the congregation, also at the end)
        Know this:
The Christ has appeared in the realm of earth.
        Behold in him:
The bringer of healing to earthly man.
Through him has been revealed:
        The Fatherground of all Being.

THE HEARTBEAT OF THE YEAR

Inserted prayer
(after Offering from the third service onwards)

Fatherly Ground of all Being
In that through the Word,
Who lived in the earthly body
The light of your clear shining-power
Has disclosed itself
To our spiritual beholding
That we come to know the divine
Through what is seen
And thereby for the unseen our love be kindled:
We join in the offering-song
Of the Angels, Archangels, of the Archai,
Of the Revealers, of the World Powers, of the World Guides,
Of the Thrones, of the Cherubim and Seraphim
Which resounds,
That you become manifest;
And through all courses of time
May there resound:
Healing is through you.

Epiphany

Out of world-wide spaces
Appeared the star of grace
To join heart's-warming
To spirit-enlightenment
In the human being.
Into the light of grace
Into the Christ-star's
Grace-bestowing ray
Our souls
Devoted to the eternal Father-will
Would enter in humility.

Inserted prayer
(after Offering from the third service onwards)

> *Father, very Ground of all Being,*
> *In that through the Word,*
> *Who lived in the earthly body*
> *The light of your clear shining power*
> *Has disclosed itself*
> *To our beholding in spirit,*
> *That we may know the divine*
> *With our sight*
> *And thereby for the unseen our love may be kindled:*
> *We join in the song of sacrifice*
> *Of the Angels, Archangels, of the Mights,*
> *Of the Revealers, of the World-Powers, of the World-Guides,*
> *Of the Thrones, of the Cherubim and Seraphim,*
> *Which sounds forth*
> *That you may become manifest,*
> *And so may there sound*
> *Through all courses of time:*
> *Healing is through you.*

Epiphany

> *From the bounds of worlds*
> *Has the star of grace appeared*
> *To add warmth of heart*
> *To spirit-enlightenment*
> *In the being of man.*
> *Into the light of grace*
> *Into the gracious beam*
> *Of the Christ-star*
> *Our souls*
> *Devoted to the everlasting Father-will*
> *Would enter in humility.*

May the holy Act of Consecration
Be fulfilled
In the upward glance of the soul
To the star
Which called the angels
To announce
To the wise of the world
The grace-appearance
Of the world's light.
May the heart's light of our prayer
Meet yearningly
The world-light of the star of grace.
And life in Christ
Arise within us
When into the soul-eye penetrates
The spirit-ray of the star of grace.

Inserted prayer

(Towards the congregation)
The worlds of spirit
Star-radiant
Announced
To seeking human souls
The right way of salvation;
May human souls
Radiating heart's love
Find the guiding
World-star of grace
In the divine-warm
Shining of salvation.

*May the holy Act of Consecration
Be fulfilled
In the upward glance of the soul
To the star
Which called the angels
To announce
To the wise of the world
The gracious appearance
Of the world's light.
May the light of prayer in our hearts
Meet with yearning
The world's light in the star of grace.
And life in Christ
Arise within man
When the spirit beam of the star of grace
Reaches the eye of the soul.*

Inserted prayer

(Towards the congregation)
    *The worlds of spirit
Star-radiant
Announced
To seeking human souls
The right way of salvation;
May human souls,
Radiant with heart's love,
Find the guide on the way:
The world star of grace
In the warm shining
Of divine salvation.*

Passion weeks

The three weeks before Holy Week

> O human soul,
> Empty is the place of your heart,
> You have lost
> The spirit that wakens you
> Longing for the spirit's
>   Awakening
> Wells within your blood
> Want through
>   Loss of the spirit
> Surges within your breath –
> Mournful awaiting
> Is the part
> Of your consciousness.

Holy Week

> O human soul,
> Burning is the place of your heart
> You live in the cold
> Spirit-forsaken
>   House of earth –
> Sorrow trickles
> In your blood
> Hope alone
> Streams in your breath –
> From a grave of hope
>   A ray of grief
> Penetrates your
>   Gaze.

Passion weeks

The three weeks before Holy Week

> O man,
> The place of your heart is empty,
> You have lost
> The spirit that wakens you.
> Longing for the spirit's
> > Awakening
>
> Wells in the blood within you –
> Through the loss of the of the spirit
> Want swells in the breath
> > Within you
>
> Mournful awaiting
> Is the part
> Of your consciousness.

Holy Week

> O man,
> The place of your heart is burning.
> You are living in the cold
> Spirit-forsaken
> > House of earth –
>
> Sorrow trickles
> In the blood within you –
> Hope alone
> Streams in the breath within you
> From a grave of hope
> > A ray of grief
>
> Reaches your
> > Gaze.

Inserted prayer (Passiontide and Holy Week)

> *Look, O Spirit*
> *Of the worlds afar*
> *And of the earth near,*
> *Not on the sting of evil*
> *In the earthly human heart*
> *Look on the tempting power*
> *Of our weakness –*
> *My self lies*
> *Lamenting on the ground*
> *Raise it, O Spirit*
> *Of the worlds afar*
> *And of the earth near.*

Easter

> *The grave is empty*
> *The heart is full*
> *Warmth changes*
> *The beat of the heart*
> *Into jubilating*
> *Healing power*
> *The weaving of your blood*
> *Is fulfilment*
> *The surging of your breath*
> *Is comfort of spirit*
> *The comforter of your earth-existence*
> *Walks in the spirit*
> *Before you.*

(From centre, not at the end of the service)
> *My heart praises*
> *The Spirit of God*

THE EPISTLES AND INSERTED PRAYERS (AMERICAN / BRITISH)

Inserted prayer (Passiontide and Holy Week)

> *O Spirit*
> *Of the worlds afar*
> *And of the earth near,*
> *Look not on the sting of evil*
> *In the heart of earthly man.*
> *Look how his weakness*
> *Has power to tempt –*
> *My self lies lamenting*
> *On the ground.*
> *Raise it,*
> *O Spirit of the worlds afar*
> *And of the earth near.*

Easter

> *The grave is empty,*
> *The heart is full.*
> *Warmth changes*
> *The beat of the heart*
> *Into rejoicing*
> *Healing power.*
> *The stir of your blood*
> *Is fulfilment.*
> *The swell of your breath*
> *Is comfort of spirit.*
> *The comforter of your earth-existence*
> *Walks in the spirit*
> *Before you.*

(From centre, not at the end of the service)
> *My heart praises*
> *The Spirit of God.*

*My spirit feels
The Vanquisher of Death
Joy is the streaming power
Of my breath
Grace is the living might
Of my blood.*

(Turning to the congregation)
  *Your word go forth
  Spirit-wakened
  From your mouth
  Christ is risen to you
  As the meaning of the earth.*

Inserted prayer

*Jubilating
In delight
Is the air around the earth
Living
In the spirit-radiant
Power of the sun
Is the breath of the earth
Christ has entered
Our rejoicing
Pulse of life.
We find
In the delight
Of our devoted souls:
What is risen in power
From chains of death
What in the light is newborn
In the life of Christ
What heals the self
In the ground of the soul.*

> *My spirit feels*
> *The Vanquisher of Death.*
> *Fullness of joy is the*
> *Streaming power of my breath.*
> *Grace is the living might*
> *Of my blood.*

(Turning to the congregation)
> *Your word go forth*
> *Spirit-wakened*
> *From your mouth.*
> *Christ has risen unto you*
> *As the meaning of the earth.*

Inserted prayer

> *The airy regions*
> *Of the earth*
> *Rejoice exceedingly.*
> *The breath of the earth*
> *Lives*
> *In the spirit-radiant*
> *Power of the sun.*
> *Christ has invaded*
> *Man's rejoicing*
> *Pulse of life,*
> *Man finds*
> *In the delight*
> *Of his devout soul:*
> *What has risen in power*
> *From the chains of death,*
> *What in the light has been newborn*
> *In the life of Christ,*
> *What heals the self*
> *In the depths of the soul.*

Living is the soul
Which was dead
Shining is the self
Which was dark
Abounding is the spirit
Which was closed.
The grave of the soul
Opens.
The grave of the soul
Becomes an altar.
Christ offers
At the soul-altar
In human spirit light
To the worlds afar
To the earth near
Now and beyond all cycles of time.

Ascension

Divine Father-Ground
You who wield among all beings:
You have sent him,
And he has confirmed his sending
Through teaching, suffering
Through death and victory over death.
He lives in earthly being,
Transfiguring earthly being
With heavenly being;
We behold with
Heart's power of vision
His elevation to heavenly being
For the sake of earthly being.
May he dwell with us
In that he dwells with you.
With his power in our souls

The soul which was dead
Lives.
The self which was dark
Shines.
The spirit which was close
Abounds.
The grave of the soul
Opens.
The grave of the soul
Becomes an altar.
Christ offers
At the altar of the soul
In the spirit-light of man
To the worlds afar
To the earth near
Now and beyond all cycles of time.

Ascension

Fatherground Divine,
Wielding among all beings:
You have sent him,
And he has confirmed his sending
Through his word, his passion,
Through death and the conquest of death.
He lives in earthly being,
Transfiguring earthly
With heavenly being;
We behold with the
Visionary power of our hearts
His elevation to the heavenly
For the sake of the earthly being.
May he abide with us
In that he abides with you.
With his power in our souls

THE HEARTBEAT OF THE YEAR

We would fulfil
The Act of Consecration
Looking up to him.

Inserted prayer

Christ's power of soul
Reveals itself
In the heights,
Into which he embodies
Earthly being.
The eyes of our souls
Behold him
In the being of the clouds
Bestowing blessing
On earthly being.
Therefore our hearts
Sound forth his praise
And may our song of praise
Follow his course,
That we be
Those who confess him
Through all cycles of time.

Pentecost

Christ sends
Into our souls
The Father-Ground's Spirit,
Who heals
As world-physician
The weakness of souls
And the infirmities of mankind.
May the Spirit who brings healing

*We would fulfil
The Act of Consecration
Looking up to him.*

Inserted prayer

*Christ's power of soul
Reveals itself
In the heights,
Into which he embodies
Earthly being.
The eyes of our soul
Behold him
In the realm of the clouds
Bestowing blessing
On earthly being.
Therefore our hearts
Praise and magnify him
And our song of praise
Shall follow his course
That we may be
Confessors unto him
Through all cycles of time.*

Pentecost

*Christ sends
Into our souls
The Spirit of the Fatherground,
The world physician,
Who heals
The weakness of souls
And the infirmities of mankind.
May the health-bringing Spirit*

Wield in the word of offering
Blessing the deed of offering,
That works
In the Act of Consecration,
That stems
From Christ's ordaining,
That is to happen
In the light of the Spirit
Who heals
What proves sick
In earthly being.

Inserted prayer

Behold the flames
They are the Spirit's revelation.
So flame the word
Of the Act of Consecration
So flame the deed
Of the Act of Consecration.
The flames stream heavenward;
They stream forth from human hearts,
Which filled with Christ
Kindle their being
In the word of praise
Filled with the Spirit
He has summoned,
That healed by the Spirit
Human souls
Keep themselves whole
Through all earthly cycles of time.

Wield in the word of offering
Blessing the deed of offering,
That works
In the Act of Consecration,
Which stems
From Christ's ordaining,
And shall come to pass
In the light of the Spirit
Who heals
What proves sick
In earthly being.

Inserted prayer

Behold the flames,
They are the revelation of the Spirit.
So flame the word
Of the Act of Consecration,
So flame the deed
Of the Act of Consecration.
The flames stream heavenward;
They stream forth from human hearts,
Which, filled by Christ,
Kindle their being
In the word of praise
That is filled with the Spirit
He has summoned,
That the human souls
Healed by the Spirit
Keep themselves whole
Through all earthly cycles of time.

St John's Tide

To the Father God
All-wielding
All-blessing
Shall stream
Our souls' devoted
And heart-warm thanks.

In ether-spaces, radiant with grace, light of worlds
Works in fullness, in ripening glory
The Father God's all-wielding power
The Father God's all-blessing might
They work in the flowing ether-light
They create in the living world of being
They ripen in the midst of the world
Into the Christ-Sun that saves mankind.

In the Sun-Spirit's ether rays
You, our Deliverer, entered
The guilt-laden seed of humanity, needy of healing
On the field of earth.

And humbly bearing
The Father-Spirit
In the sphere around his body
  Ioanes
He spoke the word of annunciation
The health-bearing, guilt-conscious
  Word of flame

His grace-divining
Word of flame
May it burn in our hearts
Longing for you,

THE EPISTLES AND INSERTED PRAYERS (AMERICAN / BRITISH)

St John's Tide

To the Father-God
All-wielding
All-blessing
Shall stream
The devout and heart-warm
Thanks of our souls.

Light of worlds radiant with grace
Works in ethereal spaces, in fullness, in ripening glory.
The all-wielding power of the Father-God
The all-blessing might of the Father-God
They work in the flowing ether-light
They create in the living world of being
They ripen in the midst of the world
Into the Sun of Christ that saves mankind.

In the ethereal rays of the Sun-Spirit
You, our Deliverer, entered
The seed of mankind laden with guilt
Needy of healing on the field of earth.

And he who humbly bore
The Father-Spirit
In the sphere around his body
      I o a n e s
He spoke the word of flame
Health-bearing and conscious of guilt
The word of annunciation.

His word of flame
Prophetic of grace
Shall burn in our hearts
With longing toward you,

Who for us guilty human beings
Have born life from death
That we may live
In pure ether-spheres
Which can bear the guiltless alone
On the glancing waves of spirit.

He who longs for the light
Who knows the light
Reveals to our souls
Light's radiance of grace;

May our soul receive
The bestower of light
The creator of light
In light's fullness of love.

Inserted prayer (after the offertory)

Aflame with the light of the sun
Devoted to the light of worlds
You, humbly bearing
The Father-Spirit
In the sphere around your body
    I o a n e s
Herald of salvation
Look upon the deed of the altar
Which blesses human beings
Which we would fulfil
Through the blessing of Christ
Announced to us
In you.

Who have borne life from death
For us guilty mankind
That we may live
In pure ethereal spheres
Which can bear the guiltless alone
On the glancing waves of spirit.

He who longs for the light
Who knows the light
Reveals to our souls
Radiant grace of light.

May our soul receive
The bestower of light
The creator of light
In light's fullness of love.

Inserted prayer (after the offertory)

Fired by the light of the sun
Devoted to the light of worlds
You who humbly bear
The Father Spirit
In the sphere around your body
    I o a n e s
Herald of salvation
Behold the deed of the altar
Which blesses human beings
Which we would fulfil
Through the blessing of Christ
Who is announced to us
In you.

Michaelmas

The eyes of our souls behold,
While in this hour from the altar
We are to experience in our heart
The consecrating of the human being:
The countenance of him, who is himself
The countenance of the God of our humanity.
So stood he once before him
Who would graciously send
Christ, our healer,
From spirit-heights to depths of earth.
So stands he in these world-days,
Clear shining, as Christ's countenance
As guardian before the hallowed offering.
The powers that would fetter the human spirit
In chains of earthly slavery
He treads under his feet,
Which are free of the weight of earth.
And from human hearts he brings forth
The free power, which can bear the earthly
Into heights of heaven, making it pure
And Spirit receptive.
Earnestness streams from his shining,
Earnestness that before the gentleness of Christ
Prepares human hearts for the light.
Whoever beheld him in years past
Perceived the stern hand, threatening,
Stretched toward the dragon's power.
Whoever beholds him today becomes aware
How for moments he changes
The sternness against the power of the enemy:
And forming his hand to beckon
He shows us: Follow me.
I lead you to the higher divining

Michaelmas

While we should experience in our hearts
In this hour from the altar
The act of man's consecration,
The eyes of our souls behold
The countenance of him, who is himself
The countenance of the God of man.
So stood he once before him
Who was pleased graciously to send
Christ, the healer of man,
From heights of spirit to depths of earth.
So stands he in these world-days,
Clear shining as Christ's countenance,
Guardian of the sacrifice of consecration.
Under his feet, easy of the weight of earth,
He treads the powers
That would fetter the spirit of man
With chains of earthly slavery.
And from human hearts
He draws forth the free power,
Which can bear the earthly into heights of heaven
Purging it and receiving Spirit.
Solemnity streams from his shining
Solemnity that before the gentleness of Christ
Prepares the heart of man for the light.
Whoever beheld him in years past
Perceived the stern hand
Stretched out in menace towards the dragon's power.
Whoever beholds him today becomes aware
How for a while he changes the sternness
Against the power of the enemy,
And forms his hand to beckon
Pointing to man: Follow me,
I lead you to higher divining

Of the deed of life and death on Golgotha,
Which working on in the earthly human being
Creating into times to come
Shall to life bring light.
That in the earthly light
The heavenly light vanish not,
Which is to shine as from the beginning,
So now and in all cycles of time.

Inserted prayer

He who stands before the countenance
Of him who went through Golgotha
For the healing of human beings:
May he lead us into depths of soul,
From which Christ sends his power
Bearing spirit into human hearts
When, in true longing for salvation,
We feel the fire of the heart
Rightly enkindled.
He who stood before the Father God
Who stands before the Son God
To him shall our hearts turn
That the healing Spirit work in us
As from the beginning,
So now and through all cycles of time.

Of the deed of life and death on Golgotha,
Which, working on in earthly man,
Creating into times to come,
Shall to life bring light,
That in the earthly light
The heavenly light vanish not,
Which should lighten as from the beginning
So now and in all cycles of time.

Inserted prayer

May he who stands before the countenance
Of him who passed through Golgotha
For the healing of mankind,
Lead us into the depths of soul
From which Christ sends his power,
Bearing spirit into human hearts,
If in true longing for salvation
Human beings feel the fire of their hearts
Rightly enkindled.
To him who stood before the Father-God,
Who stands before the Son-God,
To him shall our hearts turn
That the healing Spirit
May work in us, as from the beginning
So now and through all cycles of time.

Notes

Preface

1. Steiner, *Building Stones,* lecture of Feb 20, 1917, p. 40.
2. In the New Testament, the epistles are the letters written by the apostles to various congregations or individuals. Epistle readings in the church services were often derived from these letters. The epistles in The Christian Community, however, are new texts. These festive prayers are contemporary messages from the spiritual world. The German text was included in Steiner, *Vorträge und Kurse über christliches-religiöses Wirken,* Vol. 4.
3. Steiner, *Broken Vessels,* lecture of Sep 15, 1924, p. 116.

1. God's Word in the Sacramental Word

1. This and the following quote from Steiner, *Building Stones,* lecture of April 10, 1917, p. 173.
2. Steiner, *The Art of Lecturing,* lecture of Oct 12, 1921, p. 29.
3. Steiner, *The Art of Lecturing,* lecture of Oct 14, 1921. p. 69.
4. In a lecture of 14 Nov, 1911, Steiner said that art of the future must become conscious art. Only with sufficient knowledge of all that lives in the human soul will the future artist be able to feel the full depth of the words that comprise pictorial language.

    > For whoever tries to make spiritual science an intellectual science expressed in schemes and paradigms does not understand it. But whoever with all the concepts we have developed here – such as sacrifice, bestowing virtue and renunciation – experiences with every word what seeks to spring forth from the word, the idea, itself – experiencing what flows out of the many-sided nature of the pictures – that individual understands spiritual science. (*Inner Experiences of Evolution,* p. 44).

5. The Greek word for reading, *anágnōsis,* could be translated as *to know through.*

2. Entrance and Exit

1. A further idea – which should be elaborated – is to compare the festival prayers with the ninefold concept of the human being in Steiner's *Theosophy*. Beginning with Advent, the different members of the human being begin to be worked through and further developed. At the same time, the foundations are being laid for these parts to be developed in the future: Pentecost – spirit self; St John – life spirit; Michaelmas – spirit man or spirit body. I owe this input to Tomáš Boněk.

3. Trinity: The Trinitarian Human Being

1. Aquinas, *Disputed Questions on Truth,* Question 24, Article 15, Ad. 2.

4. Advent: Set Forth, Become Light

1. Immanuel Kant, 'Idea for a Universal History with a Cosmopolitan Purpose,' 1784 essay. Kant probably formulated this after a thought by Martin Luther.
2. Hebbel, from 'Höchstes Gebot', tr. Mary Graham.
3. Hans Jonas, 'The Concept of God after Auschwitz,' in *Journal of Religion* (1987), 67. 1–18.
4. At the Christmas Conference after the outbreak of the First World War in 1914, Rudolf Steiner indicated that 'world night' refers not only to a natural process, but also to an historical epoch, namely our era: 'Today we have in our newly beginning spiritual science first the child. Hence the Christmas celebration is so properly our celebration, and we sense that we live today in a deep, dark winter night in respect to what can reign as human light in the development of the earth, and that with our present knowledge we really stand before something that reveals itself to us in the deep winter darkness of the evolution of the earth, just as the shepherds once stood before the Christ child who revealed himself to them.' (*Inner Reading and Inner Hearing*, lecture of Dec 26, 1914, p. 161.)
5. Both quotations from Steiner, *Festivals and their Meaning,* lecture of June 4, 1924, p. 301.
6. Translated by Robert Potter. See classics.mit.edu/Euripides/ion.html
7. Clement of Alexandria, *Protreptikos* XI, 'Exhortation to the Heathen,' p. 102.
8. In Firmicus Maternus, *The Error of the Pagan Religions,* p. 97.
9. See also Frieling, 'The Four Living Creatures and the Human Being: the Vision of Ezekiel,' in *The Complete Old Testament Studies,* pp. 104–10.
10. Steiner, *Esoteric Lessons for the First Class,* Vol. 2, pp. 251–55, 273.
11. Jörg Ewertowski, 'Die Gottesentwicklung,' in Schad (ed.), *Evolution*

als Verständnisprinzip in Kosmos, Mensch und Natur. p. 119. Regarding the question of becoming in general, see Ewertowski's dissertation, *Die Freiheit des Anfangs und das Gesetz des Werdens.*
12. Steiner, *An Outline of Esoteric Science,* p. 46.
13. Both quotations from Steiner, *How to Know Higher Worlds,* Ch. 'Life and Death', p. 198.

5. Christmas: Christ of All the Earth

1. According to Rudolf Steiner, the midnight mass in a certain way summarises the mystery rites:

    All throughout history human beings actually still had instinctive perceptions of what is most holy and sublime ... And even today, we can still infer something from the fact that on Christmas Eve the midnight mass is celebrated in Christian churches at the midnight hour of December 24 into December 25. In some ways, the mass is nothing other than a consolidation of the mystery rituals that guided the initiates to seeing the sun at midnight. In this celebrating of the midnight mass, we can witness an echo of the old initiation, which enabled those to be initiated to see the sun on the opposite side of the earth at midnight. It also enabled them to perceive the universe as something spiritual, and simultaneously, to hear the cosmic word sounding through the cosmos, the word that announced – out of the orbits of the planets, out of the constellation of the stars – the cosmic being. (*The Language of the Cosmos,* lecture of Dec 26, 1921, pp. 164f.)

2. In the notes from an esoteric lesson held in 1905 there is a valuable reference to the esoteric meaning of the Christmas night in connection with the masters of the White Lodge.

    [Rudolf Steiner] next began speaking about Christmas and about the importance of festivals. He said that during Christmas the sun stood at its lowest point, that on the 25th it began to climb higher, and that during that night the Masters of the White Lodge held a meeting from which they sent forth the sun forces of the coming year to *those* on earth who yielded completely to them, who were ready to render up their personality completely and beg for strength from them. If a person celebrates Christmas in this way, entreats the Masters in this fashion, then they will send down their strength to human beings on this December 25, and the strength of the Masters will work through them.' (*From the History and Contents,* lesson of Dec 13, 1905, p. 180.)

In the same context, at the end of that year, there is a brief but significant remark about the institution of the Christian festivals going back to the masters. He states succinctly: 'The festivals are nodal points established by the Masters ... therefore, elevation of mind is important' (Dec 28, 1905, p. 181).

3. During Advent 1905, Rudolf Steiner offered a vivid image for the incarnation process as the entry into a self-built house: 'If you imagine an architect using the best forces in himself to build a dwelling into which he subsequently moves, you will have an adequate likeness of the entrance of the immortal human soul into the physical body.' (*Signs and Symbols*, lecture of Dec 14, 1905, p. 31.) This process is an archetype for the incarnation of Jesus Christ.

4. At Christmas directly after end of the First World War, Rudolf Steiner spoke about the significance of Christmas in particular regarding the struggle against the adversaries. Our gifts and talents are Luciferic, and as such, do no good in the world if they are not imbued with the Christ impulse:

> One touches upon a tremendously important mystery in the evolution of modern humanity if one grasps this central fact of the new Christmas thoughts. The Christ must be so felt, so understood that a human being can now stand before him as a New Testament believer and say: In spite of my childhood sense of equality, I have been endowed with various capacities and gifts. But they can only contribute to the salvation of mankind if I dedicate them to the service of Christ Jesus, if I permeate my whole nature with the Christ, so that they may be freed from the grasp of Lucifer.

This is referred to as the new Christmas thought:

> This must be the powerful thought that will pervade the future evolution of the human soul. It is the new Christmas thought, the new annunciation of Christ's activity in our souls, transforming the Luciferic influence ...
>
> 'O, Christian,' says the new Christianity, 'turn your thoughts to Christmas! Lay upon the Christmas altar all the differentiation you have received through your blood. Sanctify your capacities, gifts, genius as you behold them illuminated by the light coming from the Christmas tree.'

In contrast to a life that tends towards pretence/false light, the Christ impulse is the signpost for the feeling for truth, the power of conscience within us that admonishes us towards the truth:

> This is the goal toward which mankind strives through the new wisdom, in the new spirit: to find in the spirit itself the power to overcome egotism and the falseness of life, to

overcome self-seeking through love, the sham of life through truth.' (*How Can Mankind Find the Christ Again?* lecture of Dec 22, 1918, pp. 10f, 13.)

The wording of the epistle corresponds to these thoughts: Christ becomes human in order 'to save us from deceiving false light ... from the senses' unworthy craving'.

5. The exact wording varies in different English-speaking regions. In Britain the words are translated as:

> The glory of God in the heights
> and on earth peace to all of good will.

Rudolf Steiner comments on the depth of this Christmas message: 'The simplest thing is often the most difficult for human hearts to understand. As simple as this saying sounds to us, we do well to get a clearer and clearer idea that all coming times of earth existence will be able to understand it more and more deeply, and to live their way into its important words.' (*Inner Reading and Inner Hearing,* lecture of 26 Dec 1914, p. 150.)

6. In some English-speaking regions (UK, Australia, New Zealand) above the altar CMB is written instead of KMB, because Caspar is spelled with a C. CMB also represents the Latin *Christus mansionem benedicat* (may Christ bless the house). Traditionally this was, and is still, written in chalk above the door of a house that has been blessed at Epiphany.

7. In the twelve days and nights of Christmas we sense something of the eternal divine life. A great waking dream begins on the night of December 24, the 'Christmas dream'. The Norwegian song by Olaf Åsteson tells us how Olaf falls asleep on Christmas Eve and in the ensuing twelve days and nights he undergoes profound experiences in a kind of waking sleep. On January 6, the day of Epiphany, he hurries to the church to report on his experiences. He stops at the threshold and sings his song (*The Song of Olaf Åsteson*), describing his initiation experiences in grand images. He has undergone true 'nights of consecration', in which the secrets of the world have opened up to him. It becomes clear to him that deceptive illusionary light holds fateful consequences for our souls, but he also encounters both Christ and Michael as leaders of humanity, whose light shines forth, full of grace. (See Steiner, *Our Connection with the Elemental World,* lectures of Jan 1, 1912, Jan 7, 1913 and Dec 31, 1914.)

8. Steiner, *The Festivals and the Meaning,* lecture of June 4, 1924, pp. 306.

9. Quoted as an anonymous text in Rahner, *Greek Myths and Christian Mystery,* p. 148.

10. Rahner, *Greek Myths and Christian Mystery,* p. 153.

11. See Steiner, *The Sun Mystery and the Mystery of Death and Resurrection.*

12. 'No corras' in *Eternidades* (1916).

6. Epiphany: The Star of Grace

1. See Note 6 of Chapter 5.
2. In ancient times, the Greek writer Plutarch (AD 45–125) described the genius of man as a star. According to him, besides the part of the soul that is immersed in the earthly body, there is another, purer part of the soul that remains outside, hovering above the head. He characterised this portion of the human soul as a star that guides us, and which the wise person willingly follows. Rudolf Steiner points out that this image of the star indicates the emerging spirit self (see, for instance, Steiner, *Building Stones,* lecture of Feb 20, 1917). One's own star is the individualised 'world-light of the star of grace'.
3. Steiner, *World History and the Mysteries,* lecture of Jan 1, 1924, p. 139.
4. Quoted from a preliminary talk held in Dornach Sep 20, 1924, in *The Book of Revelation,* p. 223. Rudolf Steiner had revealed the secret of the Christmas star already in 1904. Beyond the constellations and their celestial star language, it is ultimately the Christ himself who appears to the spiritual gaze both starlike and sunlike in his divine aura: 'To be led by a star means nothing else than to see the soul itself as a star … But the bright aura, aglow with life spirit, is in very truth a star, is a radiant guide. In Christ, the star of life spirit lights up – the star which accompanies the evolution of mankind. The light that shines before the magi is the soul of Christ himself.' From *Selbsterkenntnis und Gotteserkenntnis,* Vol. 1 (CW 90a) notes of a lecture of Dec 30, 1904. (English at *rsarchive.org/Lectures/Christmas/19041230p01.html*)
5. Both quotations from *The Festivals and their Meaning,* lecture of June 4, 1924, pp. 302f, 309.

7. Passontide: Know Yourself

1. From his 'Logic of the Heart', theologian and philosopher Blaise Pascal (1623–62) recognised the inner connection between self-knowledge and knowledge of God in the person of Jesus Christ and formulated it as follows: 'Not only do we know God by Jesus Christ alone, but we know ourselves by Jesus Christ alone. We know life and death by Jesus Christ alone. Apart from Jesus Christ we know not what is our life, nor our death, nor God, nor ourselves.' (*The Thoughts of Blaise Pascal,* p. 225).
2. In an Easter lecture Rudolf Steiner points to the spiritual significance of pain and suffering for the attainment of insight and realisation with regard to the ancient mysteries (*Festivals and their Meaning,* lecture of March 27, 1921, p. 173):

   > The sight of pain was meant to invoke the resurrection of the spiritual nature. This figure represented something of deep significance to the pupil, something that can be conveyed

in the following simple words: 'For your happiness you may thank many things in life – but if you have gained knowledge and insight into the spiritual connections of existence,
you must thank your suffering, your pain. You owe your knowledge to the fact that you did not allow yourself to be mastered by suffering and pain but were strong enough to rise above them.'

See also the lecture of Oct 16, 1918, *How Do I Find the Christ?* which explains that we can only find the path to Christ through inner powerlessness.
3. See also 'Passiontide' in Rudolf Frieling's Contemplation on the Epistles, pp. 146–48.
4. Steiner, *How Do I Find the Christ?* lecture of Oct 16, 1918, pp. 26f.

8. Easter: In the Realm of the Heart

1. Goethe, *Faust*, Part 1, Scene 1.
2. Our blood is in its external reality at the same time a carrier of the I. The power released from the blood of Christ dying on the cross now knocks upon every heart. The pulsating blood, however, is dependent on our breathing: what we give it when we inhale and what we release in exhaling. There is a further aspect behind the mystery of the human breath. The average number of our breaths is approximately 26,000 per day, which corresponds to the number of years it takes the spring equinox to move around the whole zodiac. Is this not a sign of how integrated we are into the cosmos? A very real healing arises in us if we feel our breathing centre to be connected to the cosmos. If we imagine 26,000 years to be one year – a Great Year or Platonic Year – then one day, a 365th part of that, is about 71 years, or, the average length of a human life. Thus, we could say that from birth to death, our life lasts one 'Great Day'. In death, we exhale our soul and spirit which are inhaled by the spiritual world. If we feel into this deeply, a feeling of peace can arise from the conviction that we are integrated into the life and movement of the cosmos.
3. When Christ appears as the comforter of our earthly existence, he fulfils what was already the mission and concern of the mystery priests. In a time when the awareness dawned that humanity had been cast out of the spiritual world, it needed more and more consolation:

> What people needed when that mood came over them ... was above all something that could be put into words in such a way that the words could be balm for the souls in need of comfort. We then see something we have often referred to as

the guidance given to people in the ancient places of rites and religion, in the mysteries, come up again during a period that is approximately the same as the ancient Persian, the ancient Chaldean civilisation in the Near East. We see how this came together with the quality which the priests in the mysteries developed and which made them the greatest comforters of humanity. They became comforters. Comfort shone out from the mysteries. For comfort was needed considering how conscious awareness developed at that time. There had to be a soul quality in the words that came to people's hearts and was like a balm, a comforting balm ... And it is above all ritual symbols, ritual images and acts which still go back to those ancient times. (Steiner, *Initiation Science,* lecture of Sep 15, 1923, pp. 125f)

4. In ancient Egypt, Ka is the life-force, the power to create and preserve all living things. See also Teichmann, *The Sacred Mysteries of Egypt.*
5. Language has undergone – and is still undergoing – through a death process. It has been misused through self interest and certain empty phrases, and we must reinfuse it with new life. Language had a high point in the Greco-Latin epoch:

> Therefore, during the time when Greek culture was passing over into Latin culture, these three disciplines flourished. In grammar, man was represented as spirit through the word; in rhetoric, the human being was represented through the beauty and forming of the word; in dialectics, the soul was represented through the forming of thought. (Steiner, *Materialism and the Task of Anthroposophy,* lecture of June 5, 1921, p. 333.)

Greek people pointed to something real when they practised dialectics, rhetoric and grammar when they said, 'As I engage in grammar, the Logos speaks in me. As I engage in rhetoric, it is the cosmic sun that sends its influences into me' (p. 335). What gradually ossified and externalised was revitalised by the Easter impulse, because Christ did not speak like the scribes but like the Exousiai. We are called to take up this example:

> Such is the impulse that must enter into men. Then, in the 'chance' happenings of today they will find the courage to recognise the kingdom of spiritual law and gradually to learn to speak of it as the Exusiai, the Spirits of Form, speak in the facts of nature.
>
> The great Easter impulse given to humanity consisted in this: There dwelt in Jesus of Nazareth the power of a being who spoke with the same inner necessity with which the

laws of Nature speak in the facts of nature, from the mineral kingdom of earth, up and beyond the realm of the clouds, to the very realm of the stars. (Steiner, *Earthly and Cosmic Man*, lecture of March 26, 1912, pp. 67f)

6. The deed of Christ in turn opens the door to the spiritual worlds in general. We can only find the way to the spirit again through the mystery of Golgotha: 'This is the reason it is so important for the human being of the present time to attain the possibility of experiencing, at the outset, the Mystery of Golgotha as something purely spiritual. Then he will experience other spiritual facts, and he will find the approach, the way, to the spiritual worlds through the Mystery of Golgotha.' (Steiner, *Pneumatosophy*, lecture of May 23, 1923 at *rsarchive.org/Lectures/GA224/English/Singles/19230523p02.html*)
7. The last stanza of a poem 'Licht ist Liebe' (Light is Love).
8. '"Bliss" may, indeed, designate a state in which all worry about the past is relegated to oblivion and which permits the heart to beat solely for the concerns of the future.' (Steiner, *How Karma Works*, essay at *rsarchive.org/Articles/GA034/English/AP1962/ReKarm_e02.html*)
9. Described in Steiner, *Christianity as Mystical Fact*.
10. In Steiner, *Rosicrucianism and Modern Initiation*, lecture of April 22, 1924, p. 142.
11. Steiner, *Rosicrucianism and Modern Initiation*, lecture of April 20, 1924, p. 105.
12. Steiner, *Rosicrucianism and Modern Initiation*, lecture of April 22, 1924, p. 142.
13. Steiner, *Festivals and their Meaning*, lecture of June 4, 1924, pp. 308f.

9. Ascension: Traces of Heaven and Traces of Earth

1. Compare Rudolf Frieling's contribution, pp. 152–58, where in connection with the Ascension epistle, he describes how Rudolf Steiner developed a completely new and nuanced understanding of this Christian festival.
2. Steiner, *The Gospel of St John and its Relation to the Other Gospels*, lecture of July 7, 1909, pp. 281f.

10. Pentecost: Flame of Spirit

1. Kenney & Menner-Bettscheid, *The Recalcitrant Art*, p. 119.
2. Steiner, *The Festivals and their Meaning*, lecture of June 4, 1924, pp. 312f.

11. St John's Tide: Christ's Light in the Light of Day

1. A child's prayer by Rudolf Steiner, translation by Richard Lewis in Jones, *Prayers and Graces,* p. 25.

    My heart thanks
    That my eye can see,
    That my ear can hear,
    That I can wakefully feel
    In mother and father,
    In all dear people,
    In stars and clouds:
     God's light
     God's love
     God's being,
    Which, sleeping,
     Beaming,
     Loving
    Grace-giving, protect me.

2. For more about the ether, see Marti, *The Four Ethers.*
3. Steiner, *How to Know Higher Worlds,* p. 102.
4. This and the following two quotations from Steiner, *The Festivals and their Meaning,* lecture of June 4, 1924, pp. 307f, 310.

12. Michaelmas: The Heart's Journey to Christ

1. See the contribution by Rudolf Frieling, pp. 164–68 on the view of history expressed in the Michaelmas epistle,
2. In 1923, Martin Buber wrote a seminal essay, *I and Thou,* on the indivisible 'I-thou' relationship in contrast to the basic 'I-it' relationship. While the 'I-it' relationship is often unavoidable, it makes the other person the object of one's own judgement and control. In the 'I-thou' relationship, however, the I-sense is activated in relation to the other, thereby honouring the other as a being.
3. Steiner, *Wahrspruchworte,* p. 178 (this translation by Mary Graham).
4. In the context of human history, our current situation is such that the etheric body and physical body have become congruent and bound together. 'Early on in the post-Atlantean age, in ancient India, in the Persian, Chaldean and even in the Egyptian civilisations many people had not yet linked their ether body so firmly with the physical body that they were unable to receive impressions from the spiritual world ...' (Steiner, *Good and Evil Spirits,* lecture of April 13, 1908, p. 95). Today, a complete dwelling in the physical body has been achieved, but this has also meant isolation from the spiritual worlds. The consequence of this loss of the light of heaven in the light of earth has been absolute material-

ism: humanity is threatened not only with the loss of the memory of the spiritual worlds, but loss of the belief in the spiritual worlds in general.
5. In the last period of Rudolf Steiner's life he gave a remarkable description of Michael's earnest countenance: 'Michael is *earnest* in all things, for earnestness, as the manifestation of a being, is a reflection of the cosmos from this being; smiling is the expression of that which proceeds and radiates from a being into the world'. (*Anthroposophical Leading Thoughts,* p. 99.)
6. Steiner, *Building Stones,* lecture of March 13, 1917.
7. Steiner, *Ancient Myths and the New Isis Mystery,* lecture of December 23, 1917.
8. Unpublished recollections of Friedrich Rittelmeyer in The Christian Community priests' monthly circular at the end of 1932.
9. Steiner, *Man and the World of Stars,* lecture of Dec 24, 1922, pp. 135, 138f.
10. Steiner, *The Cycle of the Year,* lecture of April 2, 1923, pp. 45f.
11. Steiner, *The Cycle of the Year,* lecture of April 1, 1923, pp. 32f.
12. Steiner, *Pneumatosophy,* lecture of May 23, 1923.
13. Unpublished recollections in The Christian Community priests' monthly circular.
14. Steiner, *Michaelmas and the Soul-Forces of Man,* lecture of Sep. 27, 1923, pp. 12f, 15f.
15. Steiner, *Rosicrucianism and Modern Initiation,* lecture of April 22, 1924, pp. 133f.
16. Steiner, *Karmic Relationships,* Vol. VI, lecture of April 16, 1924, p.36. Thanks to Tomáš Boněk for this reference.
17. Steiner, *Materialism and the Task of Anthroposophy,* lecture of May 13, 1921, pp. 263f.
18. Steiner, *Karmic Relationships,* Vol. VI, lecture of Jan 25, 1924, pp. 14f.

Contemplations by Rudolf Frieling

1. Hermann von Skerst (1901–95), Christian Community priest.
2. Steiner, *The Driving Force of Spiritual Powers in World History,* lecture of March 16, 1923, p. 38.
3. Steiner, *The Cycle of the Year,* lecture of March 31, 1923, p. 6.
4. Rilke, *Duino Elegies,* pp. 95, 99.
5. Steiner, *Intuitive Thinking as a Spiritual Path,* (also known as *The Philosophy of Freedom*). Ch 6: Human Individuality, p. 102.
6. Steiner, *An Outline of Esoteric Science,* Ch. 2, p. 53.
7. Contained in Steiner, *Die menschliche Seele in ihrem Zusammenhang.*
8. See Steiner, *The Gospel of St John and its Relation to the Other Gospels,* lecture of July 7, 1909, p. 281.

9. Steiner, *The Fifth Gospel*, lecture 3 of Oct 3, 1913, pp. 31f.
10. Steiner, *Aus der Akasha Forschung: Das Funfte Evangelium*, lecture of Nov 16, 1913, pp. 212f.
11. See also Frieling, *Christianity and Reincarnation*, p. 38–40.
12. Steiner, 'Autumn Course' lecture 24, morning of Oct 8, 1921, in *Vorträge und Kurse über christlich-religiöses Wirken*, Vol. 2.
13. Steiner, 'The Ascension Revelation and the Mystery of Pentecost' in *Die menschliche Seele in ihrem Zusammenhang*, p. 247.
14. Rudolf von Koschützki (1866–1954), Rudolf Meyer (1896–1985) and Kurt von Wistinghausen (1901–86) were Christian Community priests present at the agricultural course.
15. Professor Hermann Beckh (1875–1937), pioneering Tibetologist and Christian Community priest.
16. Steiner, *Human Evolution*, lecture of Aug 24, 1918, pp. 50f.
17. Hans Feddersen (1903–73) was a Christian Community priest.
18. The poem was published at the end of 'Book of the Singer' in Goethe, *The West-Easter Divan*, p. 19.
19. Johannes Perthel (1888–1944), a priest of The Christian Community.
20. Steiner, *The Sun Mystery and the Mystery of Death and Resurrection*, lecture of April 24, 1922.
21. Lecture of Aug 24, 1918 in Steiner, *Human Evolution;* lecture of Nov 6, 1921 in Steiner, *Cosmosophy*, Vol. 2.
22. Julian the Apostate, *Hymn to King Helios*, in *The Works of the Emperor Julian*, Vol. 1, Loeb Classics, 1913.
23. See, for instance, Otto Willmann, *Geschichte des Idealismus*, Vol. 1, p. 572.
24. Steiner, *Rosicrucianism and Modern Initiation*, pp. 47f.
25. Steiner, *Vorträge und Kurse über christliches-religiöses Wirken*, Vol. 4.
26. See, among others, 'An den Äther', poems up to 1800.
27. Goethe. *Wilhelm Meister's Journeyman Years*, Vol 1, Ch 10, p. 177.
28. See Nietzsche's critique on the detrimental interpretation of history, *On the Advantage and Disadvantage of History for Life*. And see also Jensen, *Nietzsche's Philosophy of History*.
29 Steiner, *Karmic Relationships*, Vol. VI, Arnhem lecture of July 19, 1924. Steiner, *Karmic Relationships*, Vol. III, Dornach lecture of July 28, 1924. Steiner, *The Book of Revelation and the Work of a Priest*, lecture of Sep 22, 1924.
30. Published in *Anthroposophical Leading Thoughts*, pp. 53f:
> [Michael] liberates thought from the sphere of the head; he clears the way for it to the heart; he enkindles enthusiasm in the feelings, so that the human mind can be filled with devotion for all that can be experienced in the *light of thought*.

> The age of Michael has dawned. Hearts are beginning to have thoughts; spiritual fervour is now proceeding, not merely from mystical obscurity, but from souls clarified by thought. To understand this means to receive Michael into the heart. Thoughts which at the present time strive to grasp the spiritual must originate in hearts which beat for Michael as the fiery prince of thought in the universe.

31. Goethe, *Wilhelm Meister's Journeyman Years*, Vol 1, Ch 10, p. 178.
32. Steiner, *How to Know Higher Worlds,* p. 204.
33. Steiner, *Theosophy,* pp. 168f.
34. Steiner, *Inner Experiences of Evolution*, lecture of Nov 7, 1911, p. 44.
35. Steiner, *Karmic Relationships,* Vol. II. p. 236.
36. Steiner, *Autobiography: Chapters in the Course of my Life,* Ch 26 (Ch 57 in English edition), p. 188.

Bibliography

Bloch, Ernst, *Principle of Hope,* MIT Press, USA 1986.
Buber, Martin, *I and Thou,* Charles Scribner's Sons, USA 1970.
Clement of Alexandria, *Protreptikos,* in *The Writings of Clement of Alexandria,* (tr. William Wilson) T & T Clark, UK 1867.
Ewertowski, Jörg, *Die Freiheit des Anfangs und das Gesetz des Werdens. Zur Metaphorik von Mangel und Fülle in F.W.J. Schellings Prinzip des Schopferischen,* Stuttgart 1999.
Firmicus Maternus, Julius, *The Error of the Pagan Religions,* (tr. C.A. Forbes) Newman Press, USA 1970.
Frieling, Rudolf, *Christianity and Reincarnation,* Floris Books, UK 1977.
—, *The Complete Old Testament Studies,* Floris Books, UK 2022.
Gihr, Nikolaus, S.J., *Das Heilige Messopfer,* Freiburg 1877.
Goethe, J.W. *The West-Eastern Divan,* (tr. Edward Dowden) Dent, 1914.
—, *Wilhelm Meister's Journeyman Years,* (tr. Jan van Heurck) Princeton University Press, USA 1989.
Heidenreich, Alfred, *Growing Point,* Floris Books, UK 1979.
Jensen, Anthony K., *Nietzsche's Philosophy of History,* Cambridge University Press, UK 2013.
Joas, Hans, *The Sacredness of the Person: A New Genealogy of Human Rights,* Georgetown University Press, USA 2012.
Jones, Michael, *Prayers and Graces,* Floris Books, UK 1987.
Julian the Apostate, *Hymn to King Helios,* in *The Works of the Emperor Julian,* Vol. 1, Loeb Classics, USA 1913.
Kenney, Douglas F. & Sabine Menner-Bettscheid (eds. & trs), *The Recalcitrant Art: Diotima's Letters to Hölderlin and Related Missives,* SUNY Press, USA 2000.
Marti, Ernst, *The Four Ethers,* Schaumburg Publications, USA 1984.
Nietzsche, Friedrich, *On the Advantage and Disadvantage of History for Life,* Hackett, USA 1980.
Pascal, *The Thoughts of Blaise Pascal,* (tr. C. Kegan Paul), Kegan Paul, Trench, UK 1885.

Rahner, Hugo, *Greek Myths and Christian Mystery,* (tr. Brian Battershaw) Biblo & Tannen, USA 1971.

Rilke, Rainer Maria, *Duino Elegies,* (tr. J.B. Leishman and Stephen Spender) Hogarth Press, UK 1939.

Schad, Wolfgang (ed.) *Evolution als Verständnisprinzip in Kosmos, Mensch und Natur.* Stuttgart 2009.

Steiner, Rudolf. Volume Nos refer to the Collected Works (CW), or to the German Gesamtausgabe (GA).

—, *Ancient Myths and the New Isis Mystery* (CW 180) SteinerBooks, USA 2018.

—, *Anthroposophical Leading Thoughts* (CW 26) (tr. George & Mary Adams) Rudolf Steiner Press, UK 1973.

—, *The Art of Lecturing* (CW 339) (tr. Maria St Goar) Mercury Press, USA 2006.

—, *Aus der Akasha Forschung: Das Funfte Evangelium* (GA 148) Rudolf Steiner Verlag, Switzerland 1992.

—, *Autobiography: Chapters in the Course of my Life* (CW 28) SteinerBooks, USA 2000.

—, *The Book of Revelation and the Work of the Priest* (CW 346) Rudolf Steiner Press, UK 1999.

—, *Broken Vessels: the Spiritual Structure of Human Frailty* (CW 318) SteinerBooks, USA 2002.

—, *Building Stones for an Understanding of the Mystery of Golgotha* (CW 175) Rudolf Steiner Press, UK 2015.

—, *Christianity as Mystical Fact and the Mysteries of Antiquity* (CW 8) SteinerBooks, USA 1997.

—, *Cosmosophy,* Vol. 2 (CW 208) Completion Press, Australia 1997.

—, *The Cycle of the Year as a Breathing Process of the Earth* (part of GA 223) (tr. Barbara Betteridge & Frances Dawson) Anthroposophic Press, USA 1984.

—, *The Driving Force of Spiritual Powers in World History* (CW 222) Steiner Book Centre, Canada 1972.

—, *Earthly and Cosmic Man* (CW 133) (tr. D.S. Osmond) Garber Communications, USA 1986.

—, *Esoteric Lessons for the First Class of the School of Spiritual Science at the Goetheanum* (CW 270), Vol. 2, Rudolf Steiner Press, UK 2020.

—, *Esoteric Science,* see *An Outline of Esoteric Science.*

—, *The Festivals and their Meaning,* Rudolf Steiner Press, UK 2002.

—, *The Fifth Gospel* (CW 148) Rudolf Steiner Press, UK 1985.

—, *From the History and Contents of the First Section of the Esoteric School,* (CW 264) SteinerBooks, USA 2010.

—, *Good and Evil Spirits and their Influence on Humanity* (CW 102) (tr. Anna Meuss) Rudolf Steiner Press, UK 2014.

—, *The Gospel of St John and its Relation to the Other Gospels* (CW 112) Anthroposophic Press, USA 1982.
—, *How Can Mankind Fund the Christ Again?* (CW 187) Anthroposophic Press, USA 1984.
—, *How Do I Find the Christ?* Rudolf Steiner Press, UK 2006.
—, *How to Know Higher Worlds* (CW 10) Anthroposophic Press, USA 1994.
—, *Human Evolution: A Spiritual-Scientific Quest* (CW 183) Rudolf Steiner Press, UK 2015.
—, *Initiation Science and the Development of the Human Mind* (CW 228) Rudolf Steiner Press, UK 2017.
—, *The Inner Experiences of Evolution* (CW 132) SteinerBooks, USA 2006.
—, *Inner Reading and Inner Hearing* (CW 156) SteinerBooks, USA 2008.
—, *Intuitive Thinking as a Spiritual Path* (CW 4, also published as *The Philosophy of Freedom*) Anthroposophic Press, USA 1995.
—, *Karmic Relationships,* Vol. II (CW 236) (tr. D.S. Osmond) Rudolf Steiner Press, UK 2015.
—, *Karmic Relationships,* Vol. III (CW 237) (tr. D.S. Osmond) Rudolf Steiner Press, UK 2009.
—, *Karmic Relationships,* Vol. VI (part of GA 240) (tr. D.S. Osmond) Rudolf Steiner Press, UK 2009.
—, *Knowledge of Higher Worlds,* see *How to Know Higher Worlds.*
—, *The Language of the Cosmos* (CW 209) SteinerBooks, USA 2024 (tr. Agnes Schneeberg-de Steur).
—, *Man and the World of Stars* (CW 219) (tr. D.S. Osmond) Anthroposophic Press, USA 1982.
—, *Materialism and the Task of Anthroposophy* (CW 204) (tr. Maria St Goar) SteinerBooks USA, and Rudolf Steiner Press, UK 1987.
—, *Die menschliche Seele in ihrem Zusammenhang mit göttlich-geistigen Individualitäten* (GA 224) Rudolf Steiner Verlag, Switzerland 1994.
—, *Michaelmas and the Soul-Forces of Man* (part of GA 223) (tr. Samuel & Loni Lockwood) Anthroposophic Press, USA 1982.
—, *Our Connection with the Elemental World* (CW 158) Rudolf Steiner Press, UK 2017.
—, *An Outline of Esoteric Science* (CW 13) Anthroposophic Press, USA 1997.
—, *The Philosophy of Freedom* (CW 4, also published as *Intuitive Thinking as a Spiritual Path*) Rudolf Steiner Press, UK 1964.
—, *Pneumatosophy* (lecture of May 23, 1923 from *Die menschliche Seele,* GA 224) Anthroposophic Press, USA 1941.
—, *Rosicrucianism and Modern Initiation* (CW 233a), Rudolf Steiner Press, UK 2020.
—, *Selbsterkenntnis und Gotteserkenntnis,* Vol. 1 (CW 90a) Rudolf Steiner Verlag, Switzerland 2018.

—, *Signs and Symbols of the Christmas Festival*, Anthroposophic Press, USA 1969.
—, *The Sun Mystery and the Mystery of Death and Resurrection* (CW 211) SteinerBooks, USA 2006.
—, *Theosophy* (CW 9) Anthroposophic Press, USA 1994.
—, *Vorträge und Kurse über christlich-religiöses Wirken,* Vol. 2 (GA 343) [Autumn Course for Priests] Rudolf Steiner Verlag, Switzerland 1993.
—, *Vorträge und Kurse über christliches-religiöses Wirken,* Vol. 4 (GA 345) [July Course for Priests] Rudolf Steiner Verlag, Switzerland 1994.
—, *Wahrspruchworte* (GA 40) Rudolf Steiner Verlag, Switzerland 1969.
—, *World History and the Mysteries in the Light of Anthroposophy* (CW 233) (tr. George & Mary Adams) Rudolf Steiner Press, UK 2021.
Teichmann, Frank, *The Sacred Mysteries of Egypt: The Flowering of an Ancient Civilisation,* Floris Books, UK 2016.
Willmann, Otto, *Geschichte des Idealismus,* Vol. 1, Braunschweig 1894.

For news on all our **latest books**, and to receive **exclusive discounts**, **join** our mailing list at:

florisbooks.co.uk/signup

Plus subscribers get a FREE book with every online order!

We will never pass your details to anyone else.

www.ingramcontent.com/pod-product-compliance
Lightning Source LLC
Chambersburg PA
CBHW052137070526
44585CB00017B/1865